D1785203

Jam
and
Jerusalem

Jam and Jerusalem

by Simon Goodenough

Collins

GLASGOW AND LONDON

An outside look at the WI

JAM AND JERUSALEM is an outside look at the WI. Its author, Simon Goodenough, was given a free hand. It was left to him to select from a wealth of material what he saw as significant against a background of overwhelming social change. This, we said, was to be a look at the WI as others see it — good and bad. Committees can do many things, as the WI has demonstrated, but they cannot produce readable books. To those who have known the WI for many years, many nuances may have been missed. Only a fraction of the personalities who have built up the movement could be mentioned. In these matters we are all subject to the tyranny of space.

Yet here, I feel, we have a live and vital picture of a great national movement from its beginning to its present position as Britain's largest and certainly most widely known women's organization. In many ways it is a typically British story. It is rooted in the countryside. It sprang up to meet a need as all true movements do. It has at times been confused, it reflected in its earliest days that British love of amateurism — but, I hope, of inspired amateurism.

Even today the WI, with its 420,000 members, its carefully organized and highly democratic committee structure and its London headquarters, does not pretend to be a slick, high-pressure movement full of instant certainties and glibly confident decisions. We leave the theoretical Utopias to others and concentrate on the down-to-earth ways in which ordinary lives can be improved.

ISBN   0 00 411806 5 cased
           0 00 411807 3 paperback
First published in 1977
© National Federation of Women's Institutes 1977
Published by William Collins Sons and Company Limited
Glasgow and London
Designed and created by Berkeley Publishers Limited, London
Printed in Great Britain

And we believe we have done a lot to improve things as we hope this book will demonstrate. Our greatest achievement is to have survived, thrived and to be still very relevant in the terms of our times.

Through the WI and its many hundreds of Institutes scattered throughout the country hundreds of thousands of average women have been able to develop their natural skills and talents and have made their voices heard. We have also — and let us proclaim the fact — made a lot of jam, baked a mountain of cakes and had an enormous amount of fun.

On the serious side it is no accident that we sing Jerusalem, for the WI emphatically believes in England's green and pleasant land and believes much could be done to make it even more pleasant.

This note of social purpose is expressed annually at our Albert Hall meetings where the views of the Institutes crystallize into resolutions. Once a resolution has been approved by our annual meeting then we do become a pressure group — and a very formidable one.

Our movement began in the dark old days when women were quite blatantly oppressed. We began before the vote. Over the years of struggle we have tried — and, I believe, successfully — to introduce women into many administrative and social areas which until very recently were an entirely male prerogative. Women have been trained to take democracy and democratic duties seriously in the WI. And from this base they have become county councillors, local councillors, magistrates, members and chairmen of national committees. We gave countrywomen confidence and their contribution to community work at local and national level has been enormous and still is.

Today, times are difficult. And yet for women they are tremendously exciting since legally, at any rate, women have achieved equality. Today, in addition to all our other activities, we can contribute to the new Europe of which Britain is now a part.

Of course, we are still 'ordinary'. Of course, we still enjoy the tea and local chat at our monthly meetings and of course we still make jam. And this is why we are strong as a movement and why we have such a bright and promising future. If any young girl (or woman of any age) wants to make *her* contribution to a better and a happier Britain, this movement offers her just that chance. If all she wants is to relax and enjoy herself then she will have lots of fun. For we believe in complete people. And it is this sensible, down to earth, mass of average attitudes synthesized into action, which will ultimately infuse some sanity and stability into all our lives.

JAM AND JERUSALEM, then, is the story of the efforts of thousands of women over several generations to improve their own lot, to enrich their lives and in so doing to help the nation of which they are so vital a part.

Pat Jacob

National Chairman

Contents

Early WI members take to the road.

Introducing the WI

IF the Women's Institutes wished to flex their muscles, they would find themselves ranked sixth in size among the trade unions, nearly twice as large as the miners and the teachers, larger than all the print unions combined, even larger than the union of technical and managerial staffs and far larger than the journalists. Their roots are more representative of common opinion and the pattern of their branches over the countryside more widespread than those of any single union. If the chairman of the WI wished to visit every branch, at the rate of one each working day of the week, she would face a round-trip lasting 35 years.

For sixty years they have been outspoken in their intolerance of social conditions and their demands for parity between the welfare of the town and the country. They raise issues before government ministers about subjects as wide-ranging as all the interests of all the unions together. But they have never been on strike. The unceasing consultations between governments of every political shade and members of the WI proceed smoothly and amicably well away from the flare of headlines.

The social revolution they have helped to produce and which they have watched over with a careful eye since the First World War has not been the result of industrial action or the more exaggerated actions of women's liberation. In the footsteps of the suffragettes, they are against injustice, not against men. At no time have they threatened, like Lysistrata, to withdraw their favours. The progress they have achieved has been considerable but it has been brought about by ordinary women and by the steady process of democracy.

They have been called the greatest practitioners of democracy in this country and their electoral processes are more truly democratic than those of almost any trade union. Because of this, it is important to know who they are and how they have become such a representative force. This book traces the history of the organization and sets down what they have said and done about some of the major social issues of this century.

The WI is not its own best publicist, largely because it prefers to maintain a low-key image. Provincial papers generally – but not always – cover WI activities with some understanding of their immediate relevancy to the daily lives of ordinary people. The national press, however, has more difficulty today in probing beyond the artificial stumbling block of hats, middle-aged women and sandwich lunches. This is a pity, not because it affects the work or enjoyment of the WI but because it deprives the public of a proper insight into the organization.

The superficial picture picked up by the casual observer of fuddy-duddy matrons is no more or less true as a description of a WI gathering than it would be of any similar mixed gathering or gathering of men. But no observer would indulge in comment on the style of spectacles, the cut of suit or the apparent loss or gain in weight of the members of a trade union, business, or party political conference. Instead, attention is paid quite rightly to the contribution members of such a conference have to make to the subject for which the conference has been convened. We would all learn something if we did not allow ourselves to be distracted by irrelevancies but listened more carefully to the concerns expressed by the WI – concerns which all of us, including the national press, claim to share.

The WI grew out of jam and Jerusalem to become the voice of the average person. Members still make excellent jam and they sing Jerusalem with soul-stirring vigour. Jam may be taken to represent all their practical making and doing; Jerusalem represents what

they believe in. Their image is only confused because they don't belong to any kind of party and they are nothing to do with the church. There are several things the WI is and is not.

What is the WI?

Its members come from the country. They *are* the country but their interests extend beyond the country. They are not quaint; they are not mentally isolated; they are not bound to the soil. They may be middle-aged, old or young; they may be dowdy, arty-crafty or brightly outspoken; they may be eccentric, boring or full of common sense. They are like anyone else.

The WI is a woman's organization because it began as such before women had the vote. Their men had jobs, clubs and pubs; the women had nowhere to meet, talk or help each other. But the women of the WI have husbands, lovers, children; they discuss their work with male as well as female experts; they welcome men as guests to some of their meetings and as partners in their entertainment. There is no comparable men's organization and no other women's organization approaching WI membership, which is rather less than half a million.

The WI is independent. It runs its own affairs, finances itself and educates itself at its own college. This does not mean that it has a long neck and sticks its head in the sand.

Introducing the WI

Government representatives sit on WI committees and WI representatives sit on government committees; government grants are made available to further WI projects; links are maintained between the WI and government education schemes.

The WI is democratic. Members vote for their committees by secret ballot, so that no one feels under pressure from neighbours or friends to elect a candidate they do not want. This has ensured, with remarkable success, that no single person or faction has been able to manipulate the WI to a minority purpose. That would not be the intent of democracy or the WI.

The WI is not a religious organization or secret society. Church, chapel, atheist or agnostic, anyone can join the WI and be sure her beliefs won't be attacked or questioned. Every minority is respected. This does not preclude discussion on contraception, prostitution or the place of the church in society but discussion is undertaken in a spirit of enquiry, tolerant towards the views of the minority.

The WI is not a political party, nor affiliated to any such party. Party politics play no part in the WI. This means that they can comment without prejudice on government legislation, and in so doing they contribute in great measure to democracy in this country. Should they wish to do so, they could frame an effective social manifesto which could well attract several million men and women. As a statement of intent, it would reflect past action: not a bad base for a credible platform.

The WI is the village voice and encourages its members to speak out on decisions that affect their lives. There is probably no organization with one ear so closely to the ground and the other so tuned to government legislation. This two-way switch of information is the democratic principle at work and provides an admirable lesson in citizenship. In so far as socialism is concerned with the welfare of the individual in the co-operative state, the WI reflected the socialist ideal from its beginning and won a revolution in living standards for country people. Now it maintains a constant watching brief on those standards and the rights of everyone as individuals.

The WI is only part of life. It recognizes that few people want to be bound up totally in any

The WI in full session at its AGM in London's Albert Hall. It is at this meeting that resolutions become 'mandates' when approved by the delegates.

one thing. At the same time, it tries to be an acceptable part of life, just as it is an accepted part of the country scene. It reflects this balanced attitude among the great variety of its activities, its wide cross-section of members and the markedly different character of many local WIs. Some members belong to the 'battling brigade', some prefer to drift with the tide, some are 'loners', busy with their own craft.

The WI is well-organized. That does not mean the members are bossed around. A sound basic structure and a few simple rules have made it survive for sixty years and enable it to run its own affairs without trouble. It is one of the few organizations – male or female – that can do so. Experience gained in WI committees can help members contribute substantially to other organizations with which they might become involved.

The WI gets things done. If this book seems over-packed with incident, that is because there is so much the members have done and talked about. There are bits of social and national history, sport, music, food, plenty of jam, wartime stories, issues they've fought for, competitions, festivals, pageants, drama, friends abroad and many anecdotes. Everything mentioned probably represents several thousand similar incidents. The anecdotes are certainly only a very small fraction of similar – and no doubt much better – stories that proliferate throughout the WI. Any village could have supplied a hundred more; every person a private store.

Certain parts of the book are for the record: how the WI began and grew; some of the problems that arose, some of the celebrations, some of the planning and some of the setting in order of their own house. The dates that are spread through the book, and the 'mandates' that accompany them, show what the WI have been shouting about loudest and when. These 'mandates' are the result of resolutions that have been put to the vote at annual general meetings (AGM) and passed by the required majority of delegates of every local WI. In consequence, every WI is committed to act on the mandate. Some of their demands and concerns will surprise you. They have often been well in advance of their time.

A triple framework

There are three types of WI mentioned in the book, so it may help to get them straight. There is the local or village WI, the county WI (County Federation) and the national WI (National Federation). There are also the voluntary county organizers (VCOs). They are all part of the WI.

The 'local WI' or 'village WI' – or the WIs in general – is the group of people who put the times of their meetings on village notice boards. They meet every month, elect their own president and committee and run things as they want within certain basic principles. Girls can usually become members at about sixteen but the age limit is decided by each local WI. A local WI can start up anywhere, with the agreement of a few people and the help of a VCO from the County Federation.

The County Federation helps to co-ordinate the activities of all the local WIs in the county, suggests speakers for them, initiates competitions, and so on. All the local WIs are affiliated to the County Federation and elect a County Executive Committee whose members then elect from among their numbers a County Chairman. There is a secretary who is almost always paid. Every county has several VCOs, who visit local WIs constantly, give them a helping hand and keep them in touch with what's going on. They work very hard and, although voluntary, are trained for the job.

The National Federation has its headquarters in London and takes a broader view over the whole country. All the County Federations and Institutes are affiliated to the National Federation and they elect the National Executive Committee. The National Chairman is elected by the Executive Committee from among its number. There is also a professional staff, led by the general secretary. It is through headquarters that government legislation and WI reaction are sifted. The initials 'WI' refer to the organization, the members in general or the National Federation speaking on behalf of the WI.

The WI itself stands for the Women's Institute. One thing binds the WI together – an assumption of goodwill. As a first principle, they assume that each intends good to the other, will help the other and, if necessary, will ask for help. In her Christmas message to the WI in 1975, the chairman quoted an article in which the author came to the conclusion that by the year 2000, 'the Women's Institute will of necessity have become the People's Institute because by then there will be a widespread acceptance of all the things we in the WI stand for'.

Until and even after then – in our modern, bureaucratic, interfering state – the WI stands for the 'Welfare of the Individual'. This is the story of half a million concerned, co-operating individuals.

A world to change

IN the year of Queen Victoria's Diamond Jubilee, a year of much rejoicing in Great Britain and throughout the Empire, London and the nation were proud to accept as a gift from Sir Henry Tate the gallery that overlooks the Thames. Society, safe and well-ordered, had leisure to ignore the rumblings of upheaval that were about to change beyond belief relationships between men and women, between workers and bosses, between the state and the countryside.

A tremor of excitement stirred the imaginations of unemancipated wives when news filtered through the porous censorship of outrage that Havelock Ellis, himself a contemporary curiosity who in turn charmed and repelled, had published that year the first volume of his monumental *Studies in the Psychology of Sex*. When public news came from Austria that universal suffrage had been introduced, a sniff of political freedom promised substance to the thrill of sexual liberation.

Amid this heady atmosphere, country women were easily forgotten and farmers little cared for. Neglect by government and competition from abroad had run down British agriculture to a point of some depression. Jubilee year brought with it the first sign of hope for these disowned citizens of the fields. A Royal Commission made a report on the sorry condition of farms and farmland and pointed to a consequence of that neglect: the nation's increasing inability to feed and fend for itself. But reports alone were little comfort. Action by government on behalf of labourers seemed reserved for industrial factories not farmers and their families. The Employer's Liability Act for the first time laid responsibility and the cost of compensation for work-time injuries firmly on the shoulders of the boss. Who would pay for the independent smallholder and his family when *he* was hurt?

Such questions did not bother Queen Victoria's armies, basking in a brief, unsettled respite from their blind campaigns against the Boers or marching with Kitchener against the followers of the Mahdi in the sweltering heat of the Sudan. Not unreasonably, they had no time to remember the homeplace of another significant event that year, the small community of Stoney Creek where, less than a century before, with the help of local militia and settlers from surrounding districts, they had won a decisive battle against an American army and saved Canada for the British Empire.

There are two memorials in Stoney Creek. One recalls that battle; the other commemorates the founding of the first women's institute in the world, on February 19, 1897.

That new woman

The portrait of the founder that hangs in the University of Guelph, Ontario, shows a calm and graceful woman but Adelaide Hoodless grew up fatherless to the tough work of farm life. She also had a tragic experience when her fourth child died at eighteen months. It was a common tragedy. Ignorance and careless hygiene killed one baby in every five. Girls were not educated for the job of motherhood but left to fend for themselves and reap what knowledge they could from a system based on the priorities of men. Recognizing that contaminated milk had caused her baby's death, Adelaide Hoodless determined to change that system and save others from similar loss.

'The education of mothers has been my life work,' she said and to that end her energies encompassed many activities, from the founding of Domestic Science Courses for girls to presidency of the national Young Women's Christian Association, or YWCA, and treas-

This photograph of Mrs Adelaide Hunter Hoodless, founder of the Women's Institute movement, and her family was taken in 1887. Mrs Hoodless — her maiden name was Hunter — was then aged thirty.

urer of the National Council of Women of Canada. Her thoughts were not inconsistent with those of the Queen whose Jubilee it was. 'No higher vocation has been or ever will be given to women than that of home-maker and citizen builder,' she said and, to those audiences who welcomed her in many parts of the country, she offered sentiments and maxims they could treasure: 'A nation cannot rise above the level of its homes.'

In deference to the Jubilee, she assisted Lady Aberdeen to form the Victorian Order of Nurses. A year later she published a 'little red book' on household science. This was well ahead of its time. It contained calorie charts, chemical analysis of foods and dissertations on the value of meat, fruit and vegetables in diet. For those of us reared on the awareness of quite a different, Maoist, 'little red book', Adelaide Hoodless expressed some very advanced views when she described her aims in an article on *New Methods of Education*. Arguing against the cultural necessity of a classically based education for girls, she went on to point out the contemporary conflict between the idea of personal freedom and the organization of the social life. She quoted a writer who said that 'the ultimate development of organization is socialism' and she concluded that 'what must be done is to develop to the fullest extent the two great social forces, education and organization, so as to secure for each individual the highest degree of advancement'.

To whatever extent Queen Victoria might have approved the founder's earlier sentiments, she would not have liked the reference to socialism. If, as her successors have done, the Queen had joined the WI, she would most certainly have resigned and the sound of her resignation would have reverberated throughout every village in the land. 'That new woman', she would have stormed, as did the press and many others who found in Mrs Hoodless's teaching an unwarranted threat to the established order. 'Let her stay at home and take care of her family!' they exclaimed with self-righteous suspicion.

Her children confounded their insinuations. They called her 'a great mother', a 'woman with a great maternal instinct, large enough to include all classes and creeds'. Confident in the truth of one of her favourite maxims, she herself could afford to ignore any criticism. 'Women must learn not to waste valuable time on non-essentials,' she taught.

The pursuit of this philosophy gained her a wide reputation and refuted the arguments of her opponents. At her death, in 1910, the *Toronto Globe and Mail* called her 'one of the most widely known educationists in Canada and scarcely less known in the United States'. By then the public were being conditioned to change: in 1910, George V came to the throne in Britain; the Girl Guides Association was founded; the tango pranced across the Atlantic from the Americas and Dr Crippen tried to slip to safety in the opposite direction. (That infamous murderer was arrested on shipboard, and so became the first criminal to be captured with the help of radio.)

Stoney Creek

No doubt the energetic and independent-minded Mrs Hoodless quoted one of her maxims when she spoke at the Agricultural College of Guelph late in 1896, the year before the Jubilee. Perhaps she chose the words of Herbert Spencer: 'The welfare of the family underlies the welfare of society.' Then she would have talked on sanitation, on 'a better understanding of the economic and hygienic

value of foods and fuels' and 'a more scientific care of children with a view to raising the general standard of the life of farm people'. What she said deeply impressed Mr Erland Lee, a young farmer who was secretary of the Young Farmer's Institute of the nearby township of Saltfleet.

He invited her to visit his own all-male group and talk on her pet theme of women's education in domestic science. There were female visitors present, to whom she made the suggestion that they start their own group, not in rivalry with the men but to emulate in the home the improvements the men were taught to make to their land and stock. Tactfully, Mr Lee invited Mrs Hoodless and the visitors to discuss the subject more fully at a meeting of their own a week later. News spread fast, as good news still does among the WI, and the women brought their friends. Mr Lee was the only man among one hundred and one women who turned up for that meeting on February 19, 1897. Everyone agreeing, a women's institute was formed that very afternoon, at Stoney Creek.

Erland Lee's influence did not stop at that first meeting. His enthusiasm was as great as that of the members themselves. At his suggestion, and in order to broaden the horizon of the gathering from their own problems in the home to those of their husbands in the fields, the government of Ontario sent Miss Laura Rose, a dairying instructress, to speak to the women. Catching the spirit of the new movement, Miss Rose herself started the second WI and provided a motto: 'For Home and Country'.

Across the Atlantic

It was a motto peculiarly appropriate to the year in which the movement first began in Britain. By 1915 there were more than 800 institutes in Canada, every member an eager home-maker. But in Britain the concept of 'home' had a different ring for the song on everyone's lips was 'Keep the Home Fires Burning' and there was news from the war front of poison gas at Ypres and German flame-throwers. Europe was dug in for disaster. Rasputin was effective ruler of Russia. The *Lusitania* had been sunk and already the

Squire's Hall, Stoney Creek, Ontario, where the first Women's Institute in the world was started on February 19, 1897.

Mrs E. D. Smith — the first president of the Women's Institute formed at Stoney Creek. Mrs Smith's maiden name was Christina A. Armstrong.

civilian population had experienced the disconcerting raids of zeppelins. One event alone was of constructive interest to the farming community: in America the Ford farm tractor had been developed.

Amid this confusion, the first WI in Britain was started in Anglesey, at Llanfairpwll, on September 11, 1915, at the initiation of Mrs Alfred Watt, a small, assertive woman, rather thickset, with few looks to boast of except a broad forehead and magnetic dark eyes and, as she grew older, a head of shining white hair.

Mrs Watt was herself a member of a Canadian WI and had been one of four women appointed to a committee to advise and assist the Department of Agriculture for British Columbia in encouraging WIs when the movement received official recognition in 1911. On the death of her husband two years later, Mrs Watt brought her two sons to England and set about what she quickly discovered to be the uphill task of enthusing others with her own ideals.

She was not the first representative of the Canadian WI to cross the Atlantic, nor the first to encounter that infuriating British mixture of polite interest combined with deep-rooted indifference. Mrs Hoodless herself had visited London only two years after the meeting at Stoney Creek. She came as the Canadian delegate to the International Congress of the National Council of Women. Some questions were asked about what she had started but no one showed much confidence that such a thing would have any chance of success in Britain. Who would be mad enough to think that women had any part to play in changing the conditions of rural life!

The forgotten countryside

There is no historical doubt at all that those conditions required change. The course of the decline had begun with the Industrial Revolution and the drift of people, money and energy from the country to the towns. In contrast, agricultural communities in Australia and Canada prospered. By 1880, it was cheaper to import corn and meat than to buy home-grown food. There was no incentive to invest capital in improvements to the land and so the drift to the towns went on. Craftsmen gave up their skills and the welfare of the villages was neglected by local and national government.

Certain developments made this neglect especially painful. Even before the war public services had been widely extended, prompted largely by the creation of local education committees under the Education Act of 1902. Local authorities offered improved facilities that

13

A world to change

changed the face of the towns. Streets were cleaned and lighted; sanitation and water supplies were laid on; space was cleared for recreation and free libraries.

Labour candidates, backed by the Trades Union Congress, began to wrest seats in Parliament from Liberals and Conservatives. Socialism revealed the face of concern and the working class sloughed off despair. But the benefit was felt only in the towns, where labour was concentrated. Few had time to divert this new effort into the villages. What little was done to improve the lot of the countrywoman was done only in the name of a particular church or political party. Moral conditions were attached to such aid and in general the help was hardly worth the price.

Prominent among the few concerned with rural life and agriculture were the men, like Erland Lee in Canada, who in time became responsible for helping to establish the WI in Britain. The organization that brought them together was known as the AOS, the Agricultural Organization Society. This non-party, non-trading society had been founded in Ireland by Sir Horace Plunkett, a practical man who decided that 'farmers must work out their own salvation', which could only be done, he said, 'by combination amongst themselves'. A British AOS was formed in 1901 – the year of Queen Victoria's death.

Mr Yerburgh became the first president of the British society and Mr John Nugent Harris, a progressive dairy farmer, in time became secretary. Active support was received by the enlightened University College, Bangor, in North Wales. Colonel Stapleton-Cotton, a relation of the Marquess of Anglesey, became chairman of the North Wales branch of the AOS. Those, briefly, were the people, the organization and the place that fostered the first British WI. But the time was not ripe.

Describing 'what must too often be its unspeakable boredom', a pamphlet on village life had been written by Mr Edwin Pratt in 1904. He mentioned the good work of the WI in Canada and recommended strongly that Britain follow the Canadian example. His voice was heard only in Belgium where, two years later, the *Cercles des Fermières* was begun with healthy support and only one dissenting comment: 'I can find only one thing against

Mrs Alfred Watt, MA, MBE. She brought the movement from Canada and founded the first Institutes in this country.

them,' said a farmer to the man responsible; 'that is, since my daughter has come home, she finds things neglected in the house and seems to be cleaning all day long.'

A report to the Board of Education on the progress of the movement sounded impressed. A plea was once more included for the start of something similar in Britain. Quite clearly these threads of interest failed utterly to patch the yawning hole of official unconcern through which the village communities had fallen. Mrs Watt met with no support. There were other, more personal, reasons for this. She seemed,

LEFT: The Hon. Mrs Stapleton-Cotton, President of the first Women's Institute in Great Britain.
ABOVE: Mr Erland Lee (top picture) and, left to right, Mr R. A. Yerburgh and Mr J. Nugent Harris.
BELOW: Left to right, Mrs McNeilly (treasurer), Mrs Laura Rose Stephen, first lecturer at Stoney Creek, Miss A. Nash, first secretary, Mrs E. D. Smith, first President and an early member, Mrs Falker.

for one thing, determined to form the institutes single-handed; she failed to contact those who might best have been able to help and she failed to appreciate the marked differences in rural problems between Canada and Britain.

Success
at last

War was the spark that kindled the flame of co-operation among the women of the villages. Manpower and food both were much needed. Mr Nugent Harris heard Mrs Watt speak at a London conference on co-operation, liked what he heard and invited her to address the next general meeting of the AOS.

Mr Harris was well aware of the problems of getting the women together. They were not much different from the problems experienced by Mr Erland Lee. Women guests at an earlier farmers' meeting arranged by Mr Harris refused to speak, though afterwards admitting they strongly disagreed with much their men had said. Asked why they said nothing at the time, they replied that if they'd dared to do so, their men would not have let them hear the end of it.

Mrs Watt did not address the meeting with much confidence, despite hopeful signs in North Wales where, shortly before the London meeting, she had talked to Colonel Stapleton-Cotton's branch of the AOS and, with the Colonel's encouragement, had also talked to a group of women from Llanfairpwll. The women had seemed a good deal more interested than the dozy members of the subsequent general meeting. Undeterred, Mr Harris managed to pass a resolution that the AOS should make itself responsible for starting the WI in Britain. Half-asleep, the AOS suddenly found itself sitting on an active volcano.

In July Mrs Watt was co-opted on to the AOS staff as official organizer of women's institutes. The decision to start the first one in North Wales was made because of the interest already shown there. And, as the Colonel said, with its Welsh and English speaking communities and the divisions between church and chapel, if the WI could be started there it could be started anywhere. On September 11, 1915, the women of Llanfairpwll were reconvened in Mrs Jones's drawing-room and the Colonel's

wife was duly elected president of the first British Women's Institute.

Her election was appropriate in the light of the Colonel's confession in a letter to Mrs Watt some time later. He was, he said, 'one of the many who doubted the capacity of women to conduct even their own business with success'. He was delighted to say, however, that his opinions were quite reformed: 'I have learned more about women than I have learned in forty years. I see and believe that women can and will bring all classes, all denominations, all interests, all schools of the best thought together in that common brotherhood of love and tolerance which every man and every woman longs for in his or her innermost heart ... We want to think more, we want to understand one another, we want to think kindly of one another. We are none of us altogether bad sorts ... I can conceive nobody better calculated to make us shake hands all round than woman and her work in these institutes.'

There were those who did not agree with the Colonel's revised opinion but inclined to his first opinion. One critic mentioned 'Mrs Watt's so-called work', which was considered 'an absolute waste of money. If the movement is going to be of any value at all it will not become so by taking it up as a scheme for improving village people.'

First steps
to freedom

The tireless Mrs Watt was not to be put off. She accepted the challenge. On November 9, she attended the opening of the first WI in England, at Singleton and East Dean, West Sussex. The last surviving founder member, Mrs Norrell, is now aged over ninety. Two years later, in 1917, Sussex became the first county to form its own County Federation to help organize the WIs within its boundaries.

1917 was important to the development of the WI in two ways. There were, by then, about a hundred institutes formed in England and Wales and the WI was expanding too fast for the comfort of the AOS. When a request was put in through the enthusiastic Mr Harris for more organizers and, in consequence, more money, the AOS gratefully relinquished their responsibility to the Board of Agriculture, who

LLANFAIRPWLLGWYNGYLLGOGERYCHWYRNDROBWLLLLANTYSILIOGOGOGOCH

The first Institute in Britain was formed at the Anglesey village of Llanfairpwll – for the full spelling see the railway sign above – on September 11, 1915; on the initiative of Mrs Alfred Watt, a Canadian.

placed the WI under the care of the Women's Branch of the Board's Food Production Department. There, with the encouragement of Miss Meriel Talbot, they undertook to link women war-workers in country districts with members of the Women's Land Army. It was the first step to freedom and independence.

The next event of 1917 was the confirmation of Lady Denman as Chairman of the National Federation of all the women's institutes – or, as it is known, the NFWI. It had been decided in the autumn of the previous year that the WI should have a chairman of its own. Lady Salisbury was the first choice and declined. Lady Denman, only thirty-three, who had already spent several years in Australia as the wife of the governor-general, was proposed as a sympathetic alternative. She joined the WI in October, 1916, and immediately threw herself into the task of persuading Miss Talbot that the WI wished to become a fully independent democratic organization as quickly as possible.

The conference which confirmed her as chairman was called at the Central Hall, Westminster, in October, 1917, the month of the Russian Revolution. Sixty delegates came from 137 institutes. A constitution was adopted by the newly formed National Federation without any dissentions. From that moment there existed the three main aspects of the organization: the village WIs, on which the whole movement rested; the County Federations, who fostered their own WIs; and the National Federation, whose duty it was to provide guidance and a united structure and to which, in a short time, all the WIs and County Federations would become affiliated.

The future shape of the movement, as well as its survival, depended greatly upon the achievement of a workable structure. The village WIs could safely leave that in the capable and caring hands of Lady Denman and the National and County officers they themselves had elected. Most members had more immediate cares and joys. Village women had much to learn about each other and the world outside their small community. In those early years the foundations of the WI were being created by practical experience and experiment.

Meanwhile, the German unrestricted submarine blockade was taking its effect. At the end of April, 1917, Britain had stores of food sufficient to last only six weeks.

17

The meeting place

'WE don't know what you've got,' wrote one Kent village to a neighbouring WI, 'but we want exactly the same.' What they had, at last, was an unprejudiced meeting place, a focal point for the women at which they could voice their complaints, express their concern, give help together and make friends.

Making friends was the first and most important thing to do, as one early member recalls. 'The institute has brought together in our very rural village women of all classes in true friendships,' she wrote; 'women who have lived in the same village for many years as total strangers to each other not perhaps from any unkind or class feeling but from sheer want of opportunity for meeting and making friends. Women who have never ventured out to church or chapel or village entertainment . . . now come eagerly to our meetings, forget their shyness in opening up their minds to new ideas and welcome opportunities for developing their hidden talents.'

That radical organization

At the beginning of the century many villages were all but cut off from the outside world. Lack of transport confined activities to parish boundaries, within which villagers moved in closed communities, divided between a meagre variety of village interests, between religion, class and party. 'This is the first organization I've been able to join in the village,' sighed one woman with relief, 'everything else is got up by the Church or the Conservatives and I am a Catholic and a Liberal.'

The WI were out to cross class barriers as well as those of religion and party. But there were problems to be overcome. Resistance from the 'Manor House' took many forms, from bewilderment to outright protest. 'Meet-ings such as you describe,' said one outspoken lady, 'would, we feel, give the lower classes a false sense of their own importance, which would be most undesirable.' 'That radical organization,' said another, refusing to participate when she realized the undermining of her position which might be brought about by a democratic election.

If she could steel herself to brave such democracy, the probability was that the lady of the manor would be elected president in any case, being looked to for a lead as a matter of habit. But the new organization was determined to start off on the right foot and a bold effort was made to represent a cross-section of the community on every WI committee. One president reported with satisfaction that 'We have done very well; we have elected five ladies, five women and one school-teacher.'

Lady presidents could, however, take strong action if things got out of hand. One such, learning that a vote had been taken in her absence, nailed up her door when members arrived for a subsequent meeting. Another, explaining to a visiting speaker why the secretary and not herself had introduced the speaker, assured her that 'I *am* the president but I let other people do the dirty work!'

Discussions touched delicate topics at times. An early debate at Hutton WI discussed the arrangement of safe and respectable employment for its members: 'How can domestic service be placed on the secure footing of an honourable and desirable profession for women?' Was the question, perhaps, a tactful hint from lady president that she had a servant problem?

Church and chapel likewise looked on the movement with some suspicion though in rare cases the vicar himself might be responsible for starting a local WI. Welcome as speakers on any subject but religion, clergymen were

more likely to echo the comment of one of their brethren who said to the speaker at a meeting, 'I'll never let *my* women go gadding about the lanes in the evenings.' '*His* women,' the speaker exclaimed, remembering the incident with indignation; 'but of course they did go.'

Pot luck at the village hall

They went eagerly or with curiosity, despite the humming and hawing of their husbands. The agricultural wage was less than thirty shillings and the WI fee, though only two shillings, had to be laid aside carefully. When Branston WI started, one member recalls, 'Though people gave in their names, it was difficult to say straight off if you would join.

Institute exhibitors at Walford Flower Show in 1921. This sort of activity was typical of the fun side of the local institutes.

You didn't know how the Husband would take it, if he would let his wife go out at night. We didn't do as we liked then as we do today; the man was the Master of the House. But at the end of that first year the membership was ninety.'

With numbers growing fast during those early years, more and more village women heard of the new movement and became interested. News spread by word of mouth, though that word could be sceptical as well as laudatory. One woman, visiting her sister, was given the choice 'to take pot luck at a meeting in the village hall which may be absolutely

The meeting place

ghastly or quite interesting, or to stay at home and read a good book. Luckily,' she said, 'I chose the meeting.'

Others were pressed into service by friends and family. Mothers and daughters enthused each other. 'I'm delighted to hear you are getting on so well with the WI,' wrote the mother of one eminent early member; 'I never thought you had it in you.'

At the meetings themselves, there was work to be done as well as friendships to be made. There was a war to win – against the enemy blockade outside and the barriers of insularity at home. The combined result of this co-operative call to arms was a burst of unprecedented activity that overflowed into the full range of village life. Once they got talking at their monthly meetings and found what collective energy they had, it was hard to keep their hands off every subject under the sky.

The centre of good

Llanfairpwll set the pace, pledged 'to do our utmost to make the village the centre of good in our neighbourhood'. There were no telephones, there were dirt roads only, the doctor was five miles away by foot and the water came from the village wells. At the first meeting, there was a talk on fruit and vegetable preserving, members sang both national anthems and three wounded Australian soldiers were brought along from the local hospital as guests.

The first two years were occupied with lectures on food production, child welfare, the 'dangers of flies and rubbish heaps', with raising £3,000 for the War Savings Association, starting, equipping and organizing a girls' club and with obtaining a district nurse for the village for whom the WI made itself largely responsible and for whom it provided special bags complete with everything needed for confinement. This included babies' layettes, given out on loan to those mothers who might need them and kept in readiness and good order by the WI.

Nurse Williams, the newly elected district nurse and herself a founder member of Llanfairpwll WI, also gave classes to the fourteen-to-sixteen-year-olds in mothercraft and ran a baby clinic. With a certain degree of tact, this started off as a baby *show*, at which proud mothers displayed their offspring for praise and Nurse Williams was able to cast a critical glance at their health without arousing suspicion. All the same, the mothers were cautious. Three turned up for the first clinic and none would undress her baby in front of the others. Resistance was gradually worn down. Baby shows became one of the most popular pastimes at all new WI meetings.

By the end of the war, Llanfairpwll members were ambitiously discussing 'Bolshevism in its simplest form' and simultaneously battling for mains water and better rural living conditions. Clearly they were entering into the spirit expressed in the preface to the first edition of the WI Handbook. Grace Hadow, vice-chairman, wrote, 'Women's Institutes are gatherings of countrywomen, who meet together once a month to discuss matters of interest to them all. Nothing could sound simpler and yet to one really intimate with English rural life nothing could be more significant of the change which has permeated to remote hamlets and scattered farms, as well as to the workshops and mine. As a nation we are learning to think for ourselves, not merely to accept the catch phrase of the moment; we go about with a perpetual "Why?" in our minds if not on our lips. "Why should these things be?" And on the answer to that "Why?" depends the fate of our country, for it involves the meaning of Democracy.'

Let balance be your watchword

There was a simpler 'Why?' on the lips of others, struggling with the problems of early meetings. 'The first day of the Institute we hadn't anything of our own; we had to borrow and my Husband used to say, the next time you have a WI meeting I'm going out for the night, for it's "Can you lend us a few cups and saucers or a knife or some chairs?" You can't read your paper; there is always someone knocking.' The voice of the Branston member's husband echoes on the conscience of all her contemporaries.

During as well as after wartime, the first problem was always to find a home for the new WI, to persuade a member to lend her house, to find a hall or smarten up a disused army hut. Ticehurst WI transferred its smocking classes to the Village Club, an all-male precinct built for the village by the Newington family. But Colonel Newington was heard to murmur, 'No good will come of it'.

Then there was a table to provide for the president, cups and saucers for tea, the coal fire and oil lamps to light. There was the difficulty of reaching the meeting, often several miles away by foot and in the dark. Coming in out of the cold, the effort required made members determined to have a worthwhile meeting. They looked forward to chatting together at the social tea-break, to listen to a speaker from outside the valley talk on a subject they had always wanted to know more about or never even heard of, to learn a new craft from a visiting instructress or another member, to enjoy simple or even uproarious games, to work together to raise money to help a cause.

Through all this they learnt the sensible business of citizenship. They learnt how to run their own meeting, how to vote for their officers, how to speak in front of others, how to make collective decisions, how to put those decisions into effect, how to relate the problems of their own lives to the wider problems outside the village, how to listen to what local and national government were saying and doing and how to comment on their own actions or stir others out of inaction.

In the first annual report of 1917, there is a full record of jam-making and bottling, storing and cultivating vegetables, herb collecting and potato spraying, the formation of rabbit clubs, pig clubs, coal clubs and libraries, of goat clubs and soup kitchens, of basket and toy making, of patriotic pageants in aid of charity and the collection of thistle-down for quilts and cushions, of demonstrations, competitions, exhibitions, entertainments and roll calls, in which each member contributed to discussion.

Members recall endless fund-raising and gifts to charities: whist drives, eggs for hospital children, linen leagues, needlework guilds to make things for the poor, toy collections, silver spoons for new babies, entertainment for old folk, presents to convalescent homes. One of the most popular demonstra-tions gave instruction in the resoling of shoes with old rubber tires – a reflection on how far the members had to walk.

Mrs Watt firmly said, 'When planning your activities let balance be your watchword.' So they ensured that their priorities were right. In order of importance, a WI secretary recorded that 'we have secured a pig and given partial support to the village nurse'.

A spirit of adventure

An institute was formed at Downton, like many others, as a direct result of an address by Mrs Watt to village women. Members threw themselves with great enthusiasm into discussions on goats, bees, rabbits and hay boxes. They collected waste paper and herbs for medicinal purposes. They produced an extra eleven and a half tons of potatoes in a tremendous co-operative effort to boost the nation's larder. When war ended they began a choir, formed a folk dance team and a drama group, which gained notoriety and headlines in the local paper when, only minutes before the show, Henry VIII made her intention clear that she *would not* wear her beard.

They made rugs and raffia-work, rush baskets and papiermâché decorations and, to balance such frivolity, their birthday parties were marked by inspiring addresses on 'Women as Empire Builders'. Such ponderous sentiments did not endure. Members rebelled and put their talents instead into a 23-pound birthday cake.

Tea was always the centre-piece of any meeting. 'Often no tea is drunk at the so-called tea-time,' began Margaret Hitchcock in an article of 1938. 'It is a word for whatever refreshment is going.' Her article ran for a whole page. 'Tea-time should not be looked upon as an interval in the proceedings,' she wrote; 'it is an essential part of the programme and has its own special opportunities. It is the time to be pleasant to new members and to make visitors so welcome that they want to join. It is mixing time.'

Outings were also popular. The char-à-banc, loaded high with excited hats and a devil-may-care demon at the wheel, whisked women who had never in their wildest dreams thought

THE MANDATES

The resolutions carried at the WI's annual general meeting are the public expression of the movement's views and attitudes. These resolutions cover a vast range of themes. Once a resolution has been approved by the AGM, it becomes – in WI terms – a 'mandate' and every member of the movement is pledged to support that mandate.

Wherever possible practical action is taken. A WI mandate is a powerful pressure weapon. The WI is a movement which is organized in almost every rural district in the country. It is, moreover, a disciplined movement which has taught itself how to manipulate the levers of democracy. Once a resolution has become a mandate the movement continues to agitate until action is taken. This relentless and constant pressure can extend over many years.

WI mandates have been the motivation for many governmental and legislative changes. They have done much to propagate the national image of the movement as the 'Parliament of Women' and have helped to make the WI a practical sounding board for ministerial and governmental decisions.

On these and subsequent pages we give a selection of these mandates taken largely at random but with the aim of emphasizing the broadly-based involvement of the Women's Institutes.

NO FEATHERS FOR HATS

In 1921 ladies still wore hats. Not, admittedly, the avalanche of ostrich feathers and other plumage of Victorian and Edwardian times, but enough feathers were used to worry WI members. So they passed a resolution in support of the Plumage Bill then before Parliament. It was perhaps appropriate that Lloyd George – who of all men may be said to have appreciated plumage – was prime minister at the time, although he was to be rapidly succeeded by the not-so-vulnerable Bonar Law.

The 1921 resolution – 'That this meeting of the NFWI urges all women to support the principles of the Plumage Bill now before Parliament' – was moved by the West Wittering branch. The resolution was sent to the promoter of the Bill, which became law in 1922.

PROTECTION FOR BIRDS

The WI was sensitive about birds. In 1933 Langton Maltravers WI in Dorset, was calling for legislation to prohibit the sale of live British wild birds. WI efforts on behalf of birds culminated in the Protection of Birds Act of 1954, which gave an omnibus protection to them all.

1921 : A better way of life . . .

The years following the 1914–18 war were years of immense upheaval. In Russia, where women were on the march, as our picture shows, the October Revolution of 1917 was producing reverberations around the world. In Britain, the full franchise was not to come until 1928 but, although none of the activities of the WI could be confused with these militant ladies who donned the uniform of the revolution in Russia, the mutterings of social change were becoming a discernible voice. Was it surprising that ordinary people sought a better way of life? The husbands of the women who were now demanding a voice in public affairs had spent the best years of their lives in the trenches – like these infantrymen.

Members were also deeply concerned about humane slaughter. This was another country matter which stirred their conscience. A series of resolutions followed Cornwall's demand in 1921 that the WI should induce local authorities to adopt Ministry of Health model by-laws for slaughter-houses. Partridge Green (West Sussex), Isle of Ely and Cambridgeshire had national resolutions on the theme carried in 1923, 1928 and 1931 respectively.

Once again the 'drip' technique worked. Slow but insistent pressure brought about the Slaughter of Animals (Prevention of Cruelty) Regulations of 1958.

WOMEN JURORS

But the WI was already beginning to think of broader social issues, deeply affecting the role of women. Modern 'women's libbers' should bend the knee to the fighting spirit of the Surrey Federation in 1921 when they declared – and the National AGM agreed with them – that '120,000 countrywomen, believing that women equally with men should accept their full responsibilities as citizens in whatever way they may be called upon to serve their country, urges upon all qualified women the importance of the service to which they are called as jurors'.

The resolution went on to demand that women should not be exempted from this duty, 'especially in cases in which a child or woman is concerned either as a party or as a witness'.

But even by 1964 the WI was still fighting for a fairer jury service. In that year a Kidmore End, Oxfordshire, resolution declared that the qualifications for jury service were outdated and demanded that the law should be changed. The home secretary, the Committee on Jury Service, the General Council of the Bar and various national women's organizations were all lobbied.

Property qualifications – either freehold or leasehold land ownership or householders rated for property with a net annual value of £20 (£30 in London) – were only abolished in 1972 when the Criminal Justice Act laid down the principle that, with certain exceptions, every citizen on the electoral register between 18 and 65 should be eligible for jury service.

FILM CENSORSHIP

The WI has always been concerned with the home and family. Way back in 1921 Leicestershire and Rutland were urging an official Board of Film Censors unconnected with the trade. They demanded that at least two women

should be members of the Board and that the censorship should consider all films shown at cinemas where children under fifteen were admitted. No children under that age should see uncensored films. They returned to the warpath again in 1922, and Barton and Dunstall, Staffordshire, demanded more vigilance in a resolution passed in 1932.

These resolutions may fit uneasily into today's 'permissive society' but these women were for the most part practical mothers. And who, today, would say that their fears were not well-founded? Moreover, all these early 'social' resolutions pressed home one main point, no matter what the theme: that women should serve on public committees and should assume their rightful role in public life.

The meeting place

Trips and 'outings' helped to enlarge the horizons of the village-bound WI women in the early days. The top picture shows a charabanc outing in 1921 and the bottom picture a Congresbury Carnival float in 1935.

such a thrill possible to coastal paradises, private gardens, cathedrals and watering places for day-trip delights. 'I have all my life wanted to travel,' said Mrs Curly Brown, 'and now it is going to be possible through the Women's Institutes.' She went to Gough's Cave in the Cheddar Gorge and was heard to murmur, 'How wonderful are the works of God,' as her gaze glanced unseeing off the stalactites and settled lovingly on the electric light bulbs that illuminated the darkness. Not feeling so well, she found it necessary to revive herself from the secretary's brandy flask. 'Shame to bring the good stuff all this way,' she said, 'and not enjoy it.'

Other WIs were more conscious of the potential for which a wartime government was prepared to back them. Among these, Penrhyn, the 84th Institute to be formed, resolved 'to

help in the production of War Food'. It had been proposed that a paid official from the Board of Agriculture should be appointed as general director for Wales. Penrhyn members had no time for bureaucracy. They opposed the idea with a practical counter-attack. 'What we really need badly,' they wrote, 'is help to buy chemical manure and good seed potatoes; our land and gardens lie on the mountain side, the soil is poor and carting is very expensive.'

Penrhyn was a WI of some determination. There had also been proposals from headquarters to make the WI more democratic. 'We quite fail to see how it is in any way possible to make the Institute more democratic,' they wrote back; 'no institute could be more democratic than ours.' Having expressed itself of its clear opinion, Penrhyn played its masterstroke. Deftly, it turned its two aggravating correspondents against each other. Lady Denman was asked to write to the County War Agriculture Executive Committee to find out what precise help was forthcoming with regard firstly to artificial manures, secondly to seed potatoes and finally to farming appliances. That problem passed on to the appropriate authorities, Penrhyn was satisfied and could get on with its work.

The good old days

One year later, the vicar addressed a WI meeting at Penrhyn and voiced a common feeling. 'Now the Institutes are being used in conjunction with other organizations to help the country in its time of trouble,' he said. 'After the war they will again help to elevate and cheer lives in the country districts.' As a mixture of many different types of people and many attitudes, the mood of the WI could change easily from crusade to comedy. At its deepest, there was a feeling during and after the war that they wished to improve the country for the sake of those who had died for it and to create a country fit for their children to live in.

With the arrival of peace, the practical improvement of that countryside could be achieved by the pressure of a united movement. But the WIs had already learnt to have fun as well as to work together. There are

Jam and Jerusalem in action in the 1914–18 war. Here village women are given hints on fruit tree pruning. All part of the war effort.

members today who recall those early years for their simple joys and interests, their 'impromptu madness' and independence. They wonder whether the WI's increasing consciousness of its own collective power and responsibility are altogether for the good. They look back to the days when the WIs 'were not so concerned with putting the world to rights but rather providing village interests for the ordinary woman'.

There is the sweet flavour of nostalgia in that memory and more than a grain of truth. But the success of the WI has been its ability to combine different levels of interest and it is well aware of the contribution it can still make to the enrichment and enjoyment of members' lives – the down-to-earth fun it can still provide. Down-to-earthness has always been a basic attribute of all WI members prepared, as

one chairman remarked, not just to call a spade a spade but to call it a bloody shovel. Their problems were indeed down-to-earth, as Grace Hadow pointed out: 'The greatest difficulty country people have to face is how to get rid of their rubbish.'

If in doubt which direction to take, the WI had only to remember Lady Denman, who forced them out of their purely village concerns and made them look at national issues, but who also understood the importance of light relief. She was once heard to complain in the middle of an annual general meeting, 'This meeting is all wrong. They're not enjoying themselves. Someone ought to get up and make them laugh.' Under the leadership of Lady Denman and Grace Hadow, the WI survived its growing pains in the inter-war years.

The character of independence

WHEN the Kaiser abdicated in November, 1918, and the armistice was signed, there were those who dismissed the WI as a 'wartime experiment'. '*That* won't last long,' they said and, indeed, the problems of peace seemed far greater than those of war. The financial price to pay for four years of conflict and government borrowing was high taxes and economic tension: the pound was reduced to one-third of its purchasing power. Four million men were demobilized and off-loaded onto the employment market. Nearly 750,000 other men from the United Kingdom alone lay dead on the battlefields of France and Belgium; perhaps three times that number returned maimed, with reduced chances of finding work. On top of this, there was an influenza epidemic in the summer of 1918 and during the early months of the following year 150,000 people died in England and Wales; in London alone, 15,000 died.

Hopes rested on the man greatly responsible for winning the war. Lloyd George's post-war coalition government had power and prestige. The electorate had been doubled by the Franchise Act: eight and a half million women over the age of thirty were able to vote for the first time in the nation's history. Government administration was extended and the first Ministries of Health and Transport were established. Forestry and Electricity Commissions were formed. Despite the problems, there was a determination to make good. For two years, there was a brief, a very brief, post-war boom.

Within that period, the WI achieved its independence. At the third AGM, in the summer of 1919, it renounced the protection of the Board of Agriculture. From then on the National Federation of Women's Institutes took upon itself responsibility for the encouragement and formation of new institutes, formerly undertaken by the Board. From that moment the WI became self-governing. Forecasting 'a big future for the movement if its governing body remains democratic in practice as well as theory', the *Farmer and Stockbreeder* added that the annual meeting 'brought together what was probably the largest gathering of rural womanhood ever seen in London.'

On the 21st birthday of the WI, Lady Denman emphasized the importance of independence. 'To my mind,' she told the AGM, 'the greatest achievement of the institutes is that we have learnt to govern ourselves. We do not believe in dictators; we believe that each member should be responsible for her Institute and should have a share in the work. It may be as a member of Committee; it may be as one of those responsible for the entertainment; it may be as a helper at tea; or as a steward arranging the meeting; but the many jobs that have to be done at the perfect WI are shared by the members and are not undertaken by one or two super-women.'

At the same time, the WIs could congratulate themselves on the unquestionable asset and outstanding talents of their early leaders, women of character and distinctive mind who, as well as being far-sighted, were also able to value the simple things of life and recognize the fundamentals that could attract others to their cause – a cause based on a genuine concern that the country woman had a bad deal.

A fine stride in walking

Lady Denman guided the WI with firmness and humour for thirty years. By her emphasis on organization and the correct procedure of meetings and committees, she stamped her mark on the local institutes and provided them with a solid grounding. Wealthy, clear-minded,

Lady Denman, the first Chairman, who guided the WI for its first thirty years. On the right she is seen at the opening day of the college which bears her name — Denman College.

of independent will, with a 'fine stride in walking' and 'expert at tree-felling', her frequent impatience with the WIs never shook her absolute belief in the value of democracy. 'It is better,' she said, 'for a meeting to make the wrong decision it wishes to make than the right decision which its chairman wishes it to make.'

Her wealth came from her father, Viscount Cowdray, who, as Weetman Pearson, had built up the family firm of Samuel Pearson and Son to a worldwide contracting business. An advocate of worker participation and feminist free speech, he imbued his daughter with his own views of hard effort. She liked to win, whether in sport, which she enjoyed, or work. Her marriage to Lord Denman was overshadowed from the beginning by his ill-health.

She was such an energetic person. When he became Governor General of Australia, she went with him and, besides finding her amusement playing hockey and golf in the huge rooms of the residence, it was in Australia that she also began to show interest in the welfare of country women.

Already a confirmed smoker and a keeper of hens at the outbreak of war, within a year she found herself chairman of the Smokes for Wounded Soldiers and the Poultry Association; she also recruited for the Women's Land Army. Her interests outside the WI continued all her life. She became chairman of the

The character of independence

National Birth Control Council in 1921 and in turn first chairman of the Family Planning Association. She was among the first batch of women JPs; she was president of the Lady Golfer's Union and chairman of the Cowdray Club for nurses; she was on the board of Samuel Pearson and Sons as well as the Westminster Press, both family businesses; she was a Trustee of the Carnegie United Kingdom Trust, from which the WI received a great deal of financial help during its early years and into the present. Lady Denman was also a governor of Studley College, founded in 1898 to train young women in dairy farming and agriculture, and she was on the Land Settlement Association. During the Second World War, she was chairman of the Women's Land Army.

Most of these activities reflected her concern for the welfare of women and the country. The WI proved the perfect cause in which she could involve herself. She was a public woman of great ability but also a very private person, whose shyness and reputation for handling government ministers as if they were her servants made her appear intimidating.

Inez Jenkins, the third general secretary and author of a history of the WI, had the chance to grow with Lady Denman and found her quite different – 'the greatest fun in the world'. She remembers a warm, inspiring woman, who played tennis and squash, occasionally did Russian dances and was able, with both hands on the table, to raise herself parallel to it without difficulty.

Since Lady Denman liked people to stand up to her, their initial awe of her made matters worse. Lady Albemarle succeeded her as chairman and remembers that 'We weren't bosom friends; she wasn't that sort of person; but she liked me because I wasn't frightened of her'. Inez Jenkins agrees. She wasn't in the least frightened when she applied for the job because she never thought she would get it. So she said at her interview that she couldn't even understand part of the new Constitution. Lady Denman was delighted and explained that probably no one else could understand it either as that part had not yet been put into practice.

Liked or feared, ruthless, impartial, domineering, there was no doubt that the 'Golden Eagle', as she was sometimes known, from the

Grace Hadow, the 'intellectual' of the movement and Lady Denman's vice-chairman and partner for twenty years. She died in 1940.

colour of her hair, could if she wished control the WI with the utmost tact and skill. She was at her best at the AGM, when she addressed representatives of all the WIs and handled their debates and resolutions.

'She was splendid,' reported one newspaper. 'She never faltered. She cut short a few of the more verbose and kept others to the point; but she was always ready to help on the more modest, encourage the expression of views, deal swiftly and certainly with a few difficult points of order that arose. She held the whole meeting in her hand, yet never once abused her remarkable influence upon a gathering collected from every corner of England and Wales. By the end of the day she seemed the personal friend of everybody present.'

She was not, in fact, a very good public speaker. It was not intentional that the motto for the month on the programme of one WI she had to address read, 'Hope for the best, expect the worst, take what comes!' She did have flair and personality. She believed that a chairman should 'stand up, speak up, sum up and shut up' and she expected others to do the same. Again and again she is referred to by all kinds of people as the best chairman of a meeting they had ever known – male or female.

She was equally good at committees, in which she was able directly to impart her own sense of responsibility. 'From responsibility comes fairness of judgment, constructive criticism, appreciation of difficulties and sane optimism,' she wrote, 'as opposed to the unpractical volubility and the virulence against failure of the armchair critic.' Mrs Jenkins added, 'The complete impartiality of Lady Denman's approach to the business in hand may have made her appear to some aloof, and even alarming. It imparted to the work of the committee which she led an efficiency and a quality of detachment that were wholly admirable and uncommon in a women's organization.'

Lady Dyer considered that Lady Denman had given her one of the best pieces of advice she ever received. 'It is a good thing for a chairman to be rather stupid, you know,' she said, 'because by the time that they've taken it in, the rest of the committee will have understood it.'

The keystone of the arch

Grace Hadow was prominent on committees of all kinds. She was Lady Denman's vice-chairman and partner for over twenty years and, had she not considered her sick mother, would have had a brilliant Oxford career. She was an outstanding scholar who was also modest, easily amused and able to transmit her own self-confidence to others.

Miss Hadow was the intellectual of the movement. To her mind, the 'keystone of the WI arch' was a combination of personal self-expression and social service. By encouraging culture in the WI, she gave substance to that self-expression and set an example in social service by playing a leading part in negotiations with government departments. This fitted in well with another side of her work, at Barnett House, Oxford, an information centre on social and economic questions.

Together with Lady Denman, Grace Hadow was able to broaden the outlook of the villages. Through the WI, she said, 'members learn to realize their responsibility towards the community in which they live and, from an interest in their own village and their own country, come to see the connection between their affairs and those of the nation at large'. Between the two of them, they put the Constitution together and gently pushed through necessary modifications, patiently making new proposals to members – such as the secret ballot – year after year until eventually the members were ready to accept them.

Lady Denman used to tell a story that reflected the strength of their working relationship. It had been necessary for Grace Hadow to chair an Executive meeting in the absence of Lady Denman. 'At the following meeting of the Executive,' wrote Lady Denman, 'I very nervously had to explain that most of the decisions arrived at at the previous meeting were out of order. I can remember now my very great relief when Miss Hadow took this to be a most comic incident. She often referred to it and years after would pretend to be relieved when she had been in the chair at a meeting that it had not been necessary to scrap everything that had been decided under her chairmanship.'

There were many sides to Miss Hadow's character. One member recalls the stress she lay on the importance of language and the spoken word, on good English and dialect, at a time when the language had become slipshod and full of slang. Another remembers the extraordinarily tough walking tours she went on in the mountains of Europe. Those who knew her in Oxford might remember the railway-rug bicycling apron she wore about the town or the big yellow car she drove to WI meetings. Almost anyone who met her would recall her as the best of story-tellers, with a gift for enjoying the stories of others. Her sudden death in 1940 was regarded by many as 'worse than the war'.

Strong backing

These two were backed by the 'clear brain and fighting spirit' of Helena Auerbach, as treasurer. Lady Denman's praise was well-deserved. Today, Mrs Auerbach might have been a powerful female tycoon. She was certainly a gift to the WI. With the help of a businessman

1922: The ladies flex their muscles

From the earliest days WI resolutions covered many provocative themes – some of them with a startlingly modern ring. The age of consent, venereal disease, adult education, the problem of buses and lorries on our roads – and an agitation to retain country policewomen.

ADULT EDUCATION

The original aim of the WI's Stoney Creek pioneers in Canada was to help educate rural women. Throughout its history the WI has returned to this theme and today education in a wide variety of arts and crafts – greatly helped by the opening of Denman College in 1948 – has become one of the Federation's principal activities.

One of the earliest resolutions – passed in 1922 – showed members well ahead of their times in this area. Oxfordshire Federation urged the AGM to press home to the government the 'great need for the continuance and development of adult education in rural districts' and urged the use of voluntary societies in this work.

As early as 1912 a report by Sir Robert Greig to the Board of Education had urged that a 'widening of the mental horizon' of farmers' wives, and particularly of the wives of labourers', smallholders and working farmers, would be of enormous benefit since these women were vital partners in their husband's activities.

Sir Robert urged that women's institutes, which dealt with improvements in country life, would provide 'an opportunity to increase the comfort and prosperity of the home, help to stem the tide of rural depopulation and 'heal a national canker'.

These words, of course, fell on deaf ears, but the WI from its inception based its philosophy on just this attitude.

In 1924 the Executive Committee urged all County Councils to make full use of the opportunities for the development of adult education in rural areas afforded by the Women's Institute movement.

The 1944 Education Act made it the duty of Local Education Authorities to provide for adult education in their areas. Today, many local authorities allow time for their staff to teach in Women's Institutes. Some employ full-time teachers who work mainly among the Institutes. In some cases annual block grants are made by County Councils to County Federations to provide classes for WI members Bursaries are also provided for courses at Denman College. Between the opening of the College in 1948 and the end of 1972 some 61,000 students had attended courses there. Since 1948 the Department of Education and Science had made an annual grant to the Federation for 'the liberal education of women'. Part of this grant goes to the College.

In seeking a fuller and fairer life for women the WI has always seen education as a principal tool. There have been many resolutions on the need for rural craft education and rural 'domestic economy' in the broadest sense.

ROAD SAFETY

1922 brought the first resolution on road safety – a resolution which today can be read with nostalgia – 'That in view of the increasing number of motor omnibuses and lorries now running in provincial towns and along country roads, the Government Department concerned be urged to make it compulsory for them all to carry a guard similar to that used on all London omnibuses to prevent persons and animals from slipping under the wheels.'

This was in Great Waltham, down in Essex, where things were clearly getting desperate. The Institutes played their part in advocating all sorts of safety rules over the years. But the WI's social conscience maintained an emphasis on the

home – and on the well-being of children.

CRIME REPORTING

In 1922 Middlesex attacked the 'undue prominence being given in the daily papers to crime and immorality' – and this time the resolution pointed out that it spoke for 140,000 village women. They were successful, too, for the Judicial Proceedings (Regulation of Reports) Act was shortly passed and this made it illegal to publish any 'indecent matter or details' in court proceedings calculated to injure public morals. Alas, times change . . .

VENEREAL DISEASE

But the WI were never afraid to tackle controversial issues. In 1922 venereal disease was something nice people whispered about — and certainly not in front of the children. The NFWI Executive blew a lot of cobwebs aside when, in its national resolution of that year, it welcomed the setting up of a committee of experts by the Ministry of Health to consider the problem. And it went on to urge that 'questions of public health should be given due weight in education'.

AGE OF CONSENT

The members also demonstrated their tough-mindedness in these areas when they protested, through a Staffordshire Federation motion that 'innumerable miscarriages of justice' had taken place in criminal assault cases because of the defence that offenders had 'reasonable cause' to believe that a girl was of age. These country-based mothers were no fools when it came to a shrewd knowledge of life.

COUNTRY POLICEWOMEN

And on this same theme of control and protection the Staffordshire women were again to the fore in a resolution about country policewomen. This recorded the Federation's 'profound dismay' at the action of the government in disbanding women police'. It praised the work of the Metropolitan Police Women's Patrols, urged their reinstatement and also demanded that their 'usefulness shall be further increased by giving power of arrest to the whole force'.

From 1922 right up to 1948 the NFWI joined in a vigorous campaign to ensure an adequate women's police force. By the end of 1972 their work had certainly proved effective for there were 4187 policewomen in England and Wales — all an integral part of police service.

husband and experience as honorary treasurer of the National Union of Women's Suffrage up to the time that Union achieved the Parliamentary vote in 1917, she had the ability to forecast financial situations and the need for extra cash in time to meet the next crisis.

Inez Jenkins herself is one of the few surviving members of that early guiding group. She became general secretary in 1919. Reared on the importance of a clear and sharp mind, she was taken as a small child by her grandfather on walks of six or seven miles in the Highlands of Scotland and made to speak in Latin. She is in her eighties now, with the same charm and alertness she dedicated to her job, and the same sparkle of humour. Her saddest moment was when the WI became too large to hold its AGM in the Queen's Hall, where the intimacy of the surroundings made discussion easier and friendliness more natural.

Keeping independent

Independence and self-government gave these women great responsibility. By the end of 1919, there were 1405 institutes, a growth rate of about 600 institutes in each of the previous two years. But self-governing independence was one thing; financial independence took a few years longer. Once free of the Board of Agriculture, the National Federation relied on a government development grant to boost the institute fees. The first step to financial independence was in the form of an Endowment Fund, set up with the help of a £5000 contribution from Lady Denman on the understanding the WIs themselves would match that sum within a year. They did so during 1920 and 1921.

By raising money themselves, the County Federations gradually became self-supporting, so that less and less of the development grant had to go towards helping them. As more money came in from the rapidly increasing numbers of institutes, the grant was cut back further until, in 1927 – the year after the General Strike – it was dispensed with altogether. That year, it was possible to reduce the contribution made to the National Federation by the Counties from 25 shillings out of each WI donation to its own county to a mere seven

shillings and sixpence. There were nearly 4000 WIs.

Independence of another kind was achieved by avoiding affiliation with a number of other voluntary associations during those early years. One of these was the Village Clubs Association, with whom the WI had a stormy and uncomfortable relationship for a number of years until the Village Clubs came to an end in 1923. It was a shotgun affair. The Treasury had made it a condition of their £10,000 development grant that a joint standing committee should be set up as representative of the Village Clubs and the WI, with the intention of forming mixed clubs open to men and women. Grateful as they were to those men who had helped in their own formation, the WI certainly had no wish to open their ranks to the opposite sex. The end of the Village Clubs came as a relief.

It was also proposed to amalgamate the Landswomen's Association with the WI when the Association concluded its work of coordinating Land Army workers after the war. The County Federations themselves rejected this idea and the Association was disbanded.

Sorting out the problems

Free to concentrate on growth, the WI had already structured their organization to suit their own best interests and had overcome many early organizational problems. Two relationships had to be sorted out from the start. These concerned the County Federations and the Voluntary County Organizers – or VCOs – the voluntary workers who helped to organize the WIs within a county. The delicate balance in the WI between the centre and the circumference is easier to appreciate if we take a quick look at what was the trouble.

The first County Federations were quite separate from the central committee of the National Federation because it had been the Board of Agriculture, not the National Federation, which had been responsible for setting them up. The National Federation merely gathered them together. The counties often wrote their own constitutions and were reluctant to affiliate themselves to the National Federation and adopt the rules that the

Miss Hirst Simpson, one of the most active WI Organizers, who had her hair cut short like a man and always wore a plain grey suit. She was provided with a car to help her round the counties.

central committee had so carefully prepared for them. Many counties suspected that their freedom of action would be curtailed and much tact was needed to allay their fears.

A compromise was reached the day before the WI won its independence in 1919. It was agreed at a special meeting of representatives from the County Federations that a Consultative Council should be established 'to confer with and advise the National Executive and to keep it informed on County points of view'. This Council still meets, often twice a year, mostly in London but sometimes in a county. The Federations of Wales Conference came into existence later. These county meetings are an integral part of the communication system within the WI.

Initial misunderstandings with regard to the VCOs arose from the same source. At the beginning of 1918, Mrs Watt had three helpers in her field work. By August she had five full-time and two part-time helpers. In May of the same year, she directed a residential course at Burgess Hill in Sussex to train voluntary organizers who would subsequently return to their own counties to drum up support for the WI and help those already begun. This was the beginning of the VCOs.

The problem was that Mrs Watt had trained them and Mrs Watt had been appointed by the Board of Agriculture. The VCOs therefore felt little loyalty to the National Federation. They formed their own private association which did not come to an end until the National Federation had been independent for a couple of years and had by then organized the training of its own VCOs. These were valuable lessons in diplomacy.

Awakening the villages

The VCOs played a vital part in the early development of the WI and still play a vital part today. They are the pulse or the nerves of the WI. Mrs Watt called the course at Burgess Hill 'less of a school than an awakening' and explained how she expected her brave volunteers in their turn to awaken the villages, to 'improve the conditions of rural life by stimulating interest in the agricultural industry, by developing co-operative enterprises, by encouraging home and local industries, by the study of home economics, and by providing a centre for educational and social intercourse and for all local activities'.

One of her first classes was in how to present these aims and ideals to village audiences. The lucidity of her style comes out in her report. A lot of work was done and everyone learnt a great deal. The response to the course was encouraging, as one member described: 'No one who has seen Women's Institutes start in a county and spread like good news from village to village can fail to realize that the extraordinary response with which the idea is met comes from a deeply felt, if unexpressed, need. The people are ready, and are indeed hungry for the opportunity, and in going round to villages I have been intensely aware of the inner expectancy under the usual village stolidity, awaiting the explanation of this new thing. I have felt very helpless before it, wondering how is one to tell them about it. It is so much a question of putting it to them the right way.'

The right way was not always easy. Lady Denman's rules on the art of self-government were very precise. The business of meetings had to be transacted clearly at every level. Chairmen had to learn to word resolutions that reflected the will of the majority. Speakers had to be obtained, minutes and accounts

1924–25 : Limbering up for modern Britain

1924 saw Britain's first Labour government under the premiership of that mesmeric Scot Ramsay MacDonald, later to be branded as a traitor to the movement. Pictures: MacDonald campaigning at a miners' meeting in 1931. And England's 'green and pleasant land' – a constant theme of WI resolutions. In 1925 there was a good deal of heart-searching about Blake's 'Jerusalem', the adopted 'anthem' of the movement.

This was the era of the first Labour government. George V wrote in his diary of Labour's leader, Ramsay MacDonald: 'He wishes to do the right thing,' adding, 'Today, 33 years ago, dear Grandmama died. I wonder what she would have thought of a Labour government?'

A NEW AGE

It was also the era of the Bright Young Things, who would have surprised Grandmama even more. Women were wearing lighter clothing, shorter hair and shorter skirts. They were also having fewer children. Smaller families were the fashion and for good economic reasons. Times were difficult and within the next few years the Great Depression was to plunge Britain into its greatest ever industrial turmoil.

But Britain was beginning to take on a familiar, modern, shape. In 1923 the King attended the first Cup Final at Wembley. So did more than 200,000 of his subjects. Vast new suburbs were developing. Hire purchase was becoming respectable or at any rate acceptable. Its philosophy of 'enjoy it now and pay later' exactly suited the disillusioned wartime generation. Now even poorly paid people could afford some of the good things of life. Sewing machines, bicycles, new furniture and, of course, the increasingly popular 'vacuum cleaners'.

Britain was on the brink of the age of mass entertainment. But these were, of course, activities of the big urban centres. The greyhound tracks at Wembley set the pace for dozens of other tracks up and down the country.

Materially, new goods and products and new ways of paying for them made the average working man's lot more tolerable. And a lot of old values were tumbling down. A new Britain was in the melting pot.

RURAL EDUCATION

It was against this background that Merioneth Federation moved its resolution — carried at the AGM — urging practical education for rural life. Local education authorities, said the resolution, should be asked to ensure instruction for all girls of twelve years and upwards in 'plain cooking and such other domestic subjects as can be conveniently coupled therewith'.

The WI also wagged a warning finger — proof of their standing in these rural matters. There is a veiled threat in the last words of the Merioneth resolution which urged the National Federation to emphasize to the Board of Education 'the importance which the WI movement attaches to this matter'.

Many similar resolutions were to follow over the next few years.

Newport WI in Essex reflected the general urge towards a better and a fairer society. Their resolution on widows' pensions was also carried at that year's AGM. They urged legislation to give pensions to civilian widows with dependent children 'free from the taint of Poor Law Relief'.

JERUSALEM

Officially the NFWI in 1925 was concerned with such matters as Young Farmers' Clubs and supplementary pensions but unofficially a good deal of heart-

searching was going on about the Institute's song, 'Jerusalem'.

Why, demanded a correspondent in the March issue of the WI magazine *Home and Country*, had the song been chosen for the WI? As an allegory it was unsuitable for women. 'What woman nowadays yearns for bows, arrows, spears and chariots of fire?' 'Boadicea might have done', wrote this irate member, adding 'but that was a long time ago'. And anyway, Blake, its author, was clearly a madman.

The debate raged fiercely but most of the ladies came down heavily in favour of 'Jerusalem'.

'By building Jerusalem do we not mean trying to make life better, happier, more decent, more beautiful, more perfect, for every man, woman and child in the community? Could the WI undertake a greater work than to "build Jerusalem in England's green and pleasant land?"'

Outside the columns of *Home and Country* a more disenchanted vision held sway. T. S. Eliot published 'The Hollow Men'. But although the national mood could hardly be described as inspired a man who was later to have 'Munich' draped round his memory as a perpetual reproach – Neville Chamberlain – was in fact doing quite a lot of sound social reconstruction as Minister of Health in Stanley Baldwin's government. In some 25 Acts of Parliament he laid the foundations for the welfare state – or at least provided a transitional stage – covering health insurance, Poor Law and rating. The whole machinery of the public services was considerably extended.

For example, in the following year the General Electricity Board was formed to plan and produce a national supply.

YOUNG FARMERS' CLUBS

But the WI was assiduously beavering away in a very different area. True to its traditions it put in a stalwart plea for Young Farmers' Clubs which it saw as a valuable form of agricultural education and social training for boys and girls and also as a means of increasing food production.

The WI still co-operates with the National Federation of Young Farmers' Clubs and thirty years after that resolution was carried the movement can boast well over a thousand Young Farmers' Clubs in England and Wales.

BOARDS OF GUARDIANS

Meanwhile, the NFWI did very much reflect the reach towards social progress. Derbyshire Federation urged members to study and interest themselves in the subject of Boards of Guardians.

A woman Guardian, writing in *Home and Country*, roundly trounced the public for its ignorance and apathy. But she did note that whereas at one time there were no women Guardians, they were now to be found 'in threes and fours' on most boards and the men were beginning to realize that some of the work was done all the better for the help and advice of women.

But *Home and Country* had its lighter side. A short story meandered endlessly on. 'Oh dear', yawned Diana, 'whatever is the time?' Fanny was opening the shutters. This was the day after the Hunt Ball. The girl's sleepy fingers groped under her pillow and drew out lovingly a limp and crumpled programme. . . .

Ah, well. The old world was not quite dead.

correctly kept, elections fairly held. As responsibility for their own WIs rested increasingly on the counties, so the VCOs became increasingly important. Organizers from the National Federation came only by invitation. Interference was not appreciated.

Sometimes visitors were rebuffed without intention. 'I did enjoy your talk,' said one president to a speaker, 'but then I enjoy anything.' Another president, taking a safer line, asked a member of the meeting, 'Now, I know you would like to move a vote of thanks to the speaker'. Overcome by embarrassment, the member said, 'No, thank you'. Occasionally, the VCOs themselves were unwelcome. Usually, they were in constant touch with the local WIs but a new VCO, visiting a village institute some thirty years after its founding, was firmly told, 'We had Mrs Watt when we began. We don't want another VCO'.

Mrs Freeman, a VCO for thirty years, cycled 1258 miles in one year on behalf of the WI. Meeting Lady Denman on her first visit to London, she remembers being told by her not to look so frightened: 'We are not going to eat you.' She asked what use she could be on the Committee, since she was wholly uneducated. 'You can be as much use as any of us,' said Lady Denman. 'Education doesn't mean a thing. It is experience that counts. We go down the village streets and see all the nice doorways but we don't know what goes on behind them. This is what you can tell us.'

Conflicting views

When Mrs Watt returned to Canada to concentrate attention on creating an international association of countrywomen, there were 89 VCOs in 26 counties. The National Federation was on a firm foundation.

According to Mrs Dorothy Drage, who knew her well, Mrs Watt was 'already at the top of the mountain' while 'everyone else was at the foothills'. Without her, there is no doubt that the WI would have taken a lot longer to reach England. Lady Denman would never have *started* the WI, though she ran it superbly. It was the clash between these two personalities – the idealist and the organizer – that caused some of the early creative tension of the WI.

Mrs Watt was not wholly able to understand the differences between the WI in Canada and Britain. In 1915, at Llanfairpwll, she praised the Canadian movement: 'Simply as a result of pressure, brought by this movement, the education of our women and our girls has been completely *revolutionized*!' But the Canadian WI aimed chiefly to improve the home and create home-makers, whereas in Britain the WI had the responsibility of improving conditions not only in the entire village but in the countryside as well.

Conflict occurred at local level, too. Mrs Watt addressed a meeting in North Wales and glowered at Lady Stanley who sat knitting as she always did at meetings. Mrs Watt struggled with her indignation; Lady Stanley knitted on. Finally Mrs Watt exploded. 'I am not used to people knitting,' she said, 'while I am talking.'

Women of great character

On Mrs Watt's departure, Mrs Nugent Harris, whose husband we met earlier, took over the running of the VCO schools. Mrs Harris could not stand pomposity of any kind and would gently pull the leg of any committee member who tried to show off. Since she had a glass eye, no one quite knew who was the victim. Irish, extrovert, a good speaker able to take the seriousness out of anything, she was very different from Lady Denman. Mrs Otter, who helped with handicrafts, remembers receiving congratulations from Mrs Harris on her husband's bishopric. 'And *what* a leg for a gaiter,' added Mrs Harris.

One of the most active of the regularly paid organizers under her direction was Miss Hirst Simpson, who was given the task of preparing a syllabus for teaching the committee officers in the WIs. Miss Simpson was much loved and worked very hard. She wore her hair cut short like a man and no one saw her in anything but a plain grey suit and white blouse. Women expected her to give up her seat on public transport. Tradition had it that beneath this masculine exterior she wore the fluffiest of underwear but there was no evidence to support the theory.

She was a masterful story-teller. Her favourite tale was of a night spent in the house of

Miss Alice Williams (left), first editor of Home and Country, *the WI's own magazine, with Mrs Nugent Harris, Chief Organizer and her successor at* Home and Country, *at the AGM in 1950.*

Another time, Mrs Otter met her on the stairs at headquarters. 'What are *you* doing here?' she barked. 'Handicrafts Committee,' admitted Mrs Otter. 'Much better talk about potatoes,' came the gruff reply. It was said that she used to ride a white horse up and down the potato rows, although in time she was provided with a very small car to help her about her work.

A car would have been an undreamed-of luxury for most of the voluntary organizers. More often, like Mrs Freeman, they had a bicycle and pedalled up to fifteen or twenty miles to meetings through mud and rain, sunshine, dusk and dark. Occasionally, there was the reward, distant in the northern sky, of the dim fantastic glow of the aurora borealis.

Members on their way to meetings had similar experiences as month by month they gave substance at their own level to the movement so busily shaping itself. The fabric of the WI was further strengthened by informal voluntary meetings between institutes in the form of groups. Originally regarded somewhat dubiously by the National Federation, they remained a pleasant extra-curricula activity outside the Constitution and have become a regular feature in many counties.

It was Mrs Watt who pronounced on the shape of the WI in July, 1922: 'The Institutes stand for Fellowship, the groups for Mutual Help, the County Federations for Co-Partnership, the National Federation for Unity and the International Federation, which may shortly come, for Peace.'

In 1922, Peace already seemed threatened. Abroad, Mussolini was elected prime minister of Italy; Stalin became general secretary of the Communist Party; in India, Gandhi's civil disobedience campaign was at its height. At home, there were well over two million unemployed and Lloyd George's coalition government gave way to party politics once more. John Galsworthy's *Forsyte Saga* was published that year and so was Eliot's *The Waste Land* and Joyce's *Ulysses*. *The Waste Land* reflected the emptiness of the times and the rough vulgarity of *Ulysses* was considered unprintable. 1922 was also, until 1969, the year of the last recorded case of rabies in Britain, which creates a timely link with one of the most recent concerns of the WI and of the nation.

a WI member whose husband had eccentric habits. In the middle of the night she was woken by a knock on the door. A man-servant announced, 'Master says its time to change beds'. Curious, Miss Simpson dutifully went into the corridor where the entire household, also in their nightshirts, were wandering from room to room. She slept the rest of the night in the Master's bed, while he moved into hers.

Mrs Otter remembers that Miss Simpson was considered 'bad for our morals', and Mrs Harris kept a watchful eye on her when laughter at meals became too loud. But, of course, that was 'all part of the fun'. Once when Miss Simpson visited Mrs Otter, she was taken round the garden, knee-high in undergrowth. 'I'm afraid the raspberries are particularly full of weeds,' said Mrs Otter, a little nervous. 'Never mind,' said the large and confident Miss Simpson, 'you'll tread it all down when you pick them.'

Campaigns and jubilees

THE WI grew for three good reasons and with one overwhelming result which in turn caused further growth. It filled a need, it was well organized and it was determined to succeed. The result was to unleash an irresistible torrent of activity and to provoke the flow of an ocean of discussion at every level. Eager to share their news, their problems and their joys, the voices of the villages were quickly raised in every quarter where they might be heard. There was not an aspect of non-party village discussion nor a single subject of non-sectarian village life that did not interest the women of the WI. It grew by action and by word of mouth.

Home and Country

Word of mouth was given form, and news shared more swiftly, by the appearance in the year of independence, 1919, of the WI's own magazine. *Home and Country* took its name from the motto of the movement. It was started by Alice Williams, a Welsh bard and Honorary Secretary of the National Federation for its first year, who had written a patriotic play called *Britannia* which had been performed professionally and from which she gave the royalties to sponsor the magazine. A committee member, probably Lady Denman, guaranteed £10 and a bold first print of 3000 copies was ordered for March.

There was no guarantee that the WI members wanted the magazine but the formula could hardly fail. There was a picture on the front cover of Queen Mary and Princess Mary. Then there were seven further pages of recipes, reports from local WIs and a poem. By June the circulation had doubled and since that first issue not a month has gone by in which the magazine has not appeared.

By 1927, circulation was 50,000. By the year after the end of the Second World War, it was 100,000. It reached 150,000 copies in 1964. Even in the worst year of the slump of 1931 and 1932, when many advertisers cancelled, *Home and Country* was able to hand over a profit of £550 to the National Federation, to which all its profits are passed.

Inflation in the mid-1970s necessitated a rising price which caused a drop in subscrition to about 100,000. But readership began picking up again and the magazine took on an immediacy of approach under the editorship of Peggy Mitchell, who would like to see it tackling national and county issues at the grass-roots level the WI understand so well.

The magazine has had its share of well-known contributors but one of its greatest claims to fame is that it was once used to give Albert Schweitzer lessons in English. Returning by ship with the doctor from Lambarene, Margaret Deneke found it to be the only English text available. She used to read him light articles and advertisements in the evening, as relaxation from work.

George Bernard Shaw was asked to contribute but said it would bring about the end of *Home and Country* if he wrote what he thought of the WI. He could not be persuaded to take the risk.

What sold the magazine, of course, was the exchange of information and the news of WI and county activity. What was everyone else doing? How were they getting on? What, for instance, was the story behind the report of January 4, 1920: 'King's Langley has a social. Men invited. Husbands for choice.'? At what crafts were others trying their hands? What demonstrations, talks and exhibitions were being enjoyed?

Articles of interest appeared on every aspect of WI activity, on subjects at home and abroad,

Princess Elizabeth and Princess Margaret Rose with King George VI and Queen Elizabeth after their Coronation in 1937. The Royal Family has always been interested in WI affairs.

on matters concerning local organization and national government. *Home and Country* both encouraged and reflected points of interest and discussion. There were nature notes, a series of articles on our great industries, reports of current national events. In the same issue, an article on infant welfare rubs shoulders with a discussion on the League of Nations, the curing of rabbit skins, concerts and an essay on 'My favourite house'. There were articles on singing and drama, on international affairs, on social questions, on the environment. In 1922, the Current Events column informed the WI on reparations, peace, the coercion of wives, the law of property bill, separation and maintenance orders, the children of unmarried

parents bill, teachers' pensions, the engineering dispute and the situation in Ireland, where civil war had broken out.

Never insular, the magazine contained reports on matters of interest in other countries: an Albanian village wedding, a Danish poultry farm, Krakatoa, the Eastern Carpathian people, housekeeping among the headhunters of Papua, life in rural America, a Maori WI and Laplanders. Articles on 17th-century art, the fight against potato eelworm, the coronation, difficult children, playing cards, pig marketing,

39

the history of scent, the migration of birds, thatching, musicians, the night sky and health insurance appeared alongside reports of the latest WI outings, personalities and decisions.

Getting things done

To talk and read was not enough for the WI. *Home and Country* might generate discussion but the WI had been founded not simply to educate and enjoy itself but to press for a better standard of living for country women. Action was required and, because many felt that through this new organization things might at last get done, the number of early members increased rapidly.

They had two choices. Either they could do something themselves – keep a footpath open, raise money to buy coal for old-age pensioners, organize a library for the village. Or they could put collective pressure on an official who had the power and the responsibility to do it for them – provide public transport, look after the interests of the sick, the young and the old, ensure that country districts received the same benefits of education and health as the towns.

It was not enough merely to nag. They needed to discover what was wrong, present their evidence to the right quarter and press for action. If it was a local matter, like an inconvenient turnstile in a public lavatory or a disgusting railway waiting-room, then the village WI could write to the local council. If it was a wider issue, like the provision of rural domestic instructresses within the county, then the village WI could put pressure on county officials through its County Federation. If it was a national issue, such as widows' pensions, family planning or environmental pollution, then it could be presented through the National Federation who would press for action through the appropriate government ministry.

Issues frequently overlapped. Local issues took on wider implications when raised by many village WIs around the country. This was the case with station waiting-rooms and public lavatories. These issues were therefore brought to the attention of the National Federation.

National pressure is applied in the form of resolutions put up to the Consultative Council by County Federations or village WIs. The Consultative Council then recommends certain resolutions to the National Executive Committee. If selected, the resolution is then discussed at the AGM and voted on. This now takes place at the Albert Hall, where nearly 5000 members each represent two village WIs. This is necessary because of the limitations of space. There is no convenient hall large enough to hold a delegate from every WI. If passed by a two-thirds majority, the resolution then becomes a mandate, which means that it becomes mandatory on all WIs to work towards carrying out the proposal. Where relevant, the decision of the meeting is passed on by the National Federation to government level. The mandate carries with it the considerable weight of nearly half a million concerned country women.

There are always a great number of resolutions to be whittled down to the short list presented at the AGM. In 1961, for instance, there were 145 for the Consultative Council to consider. Lady Dyer warned the members of the Council, 'No doubt I should handle you with care but there *are* 145 resolutions and I know you will stand rough treatment.' Such was the efficiency and ruthlessness of the Council that year that they spent an average of one and a half minutes discussing each resolution. This does not mean that the resolutions were merely dismissed without thought. Such economy of time is typical of the WI. Delegates at the AGM who wish to comment on Resolutions are requested to limit their speech to two minutes, in which time, if they are succinct, they can make their point clearly.

In this and other ways the WI provides government with a barometer of public opinion. The rising pressure of the barometer has often jolted government into action. Ministerial departments take frequent checks on it, treating the WI with some considerable respect. In turn, the WI has often been asked by government to research information and opinion in the country or to publicize government action. Such research and publicity may often be more easily undertaken by the WI with its widely representative membership than by

Queen Mary, then the Queen Mother, visiting the Fruit Preservation Centre at Kemble, Gloucestershire, during the Second World War. She showed great interest in the WI war effort.

George promised support for the farm labourer's wage but by the end of 1922 wheat prices were down by half and milk prices, too, were lowered. Prices continued to fall, stabilized briefly and then, with the Great Depression, dropped to their pre-war level.

During the fall in prices, the 1924 Agricultural Wages Act did something to protect the labourer's income but there was still a large gap between farm and town wages. Even so, employers still sought to reduce their bill and between the wars the number of agricultural workers fell by thirty per cent. Four million acres of arable land were converted to grass.

The atmosphere of depression and neglect was not alleviated until the Agricultural Marketing Act of 1931, which provided for marketing boards of producers to grade and sell agricultural produce and which the WI themselves backed with their own markets. Over the next few years there were special tariffs and subsidies for milk, bacon, hops and potatoes as well as acreage subsidies for crops such as barley, oats and sugar beet. But this minimal assistance was small inducement for anyone to remain in the villages.

During the 1920s there was a large shift of the population toward the towns and in particular toward the Home Counties and London itself. London grew by double the figure of national population growth and, by 1931, contained one-fifth of the population of England and Wales. There was ribbon development along the main roads and bigger and bigger housing estates were planned. There was also much unplanned building. The first Labour government of 1924, under Ramsay MacDonald, determined to produce two and a half million homes by 1939 but the building boom did not actually begin until MacDonald's National government of the 1930s. In any case, it held few benefits for country people.

MacDonald and the Conservative Baldwin took the premiership in turns throughout this period. When his turn came, Baldwin and his minister of health, future prime minister, Neville Chamberlain, undertook some social plumbing in the shape of a series of reforms that affected the poor law, smoke abatement, the rates and national insurance, and that extended health insurance and pensions schemes, as well as controlling proprietory

local or London officials. In most cases the WI has been as happy to help as in other cases it has been quick to protest. Thus the WI acts as a two-way receiver between government and country.

In her history of the WI, Mrs Jenkins recognized three main areas of discussion on national issues. These covered the problems of *women* in particular, such as equality of pay and opportunity and the welfare of their children; the problems of living in the *country*, such as communications, farming, planning and preservation; and the problems of these two combined in the *country woman* as opposed to the townswoman, such as the production of food, agricultural education and the particular problems of childbirth in isolated country districts.

The state of the nation

National issues were not to be taken lightly during the 1920s and 1930s. The background to the country woman's problems was the social history of the time. At the end of the war Lloyd

1926–27 : A nation on the brink

1926 was the year of the General Strike. Britain seemed on the brink of revolution. But the threat (never very real) petered out and Britain plodded on into the hungry thirties. Pictures: Troops marching down East India Dock Road in London, flanked by the unemployed. And a minor skirmish in the same area.

National Savings, school meals and milk, health of the school child, care of the teeth, national health . . . these were the themes that bothered the WI, while in towns and country houses the typical Twenties Girl (according to Cecil Beaton) bobbed along in a short, tubular dress, sported a cigarette in a long tubular holder, plucked her eyebrows, wore bands of diamond bracelets from wrist to elbow and sported earrings hanging like fuscias.

Alas, not every girl could follow the fashion. In that same world whole families were living on fifteen shillings a week. There were around two million people on the dole. Prime Minister Baldwin seemed unconcerned. He puffed away at his pipe, settled cosily down in the Commons and drifted easily into slumber during foreign affairs debates. 'Wake me up when he's finished,' was his usual remark to his neighbours. But things were happening, nevertheless.

The BBC was incorporated. ICI was formed. Binnie Hale only the year before had trooped on stage with the chorus *all* wearing bathing dresses — a great breakthrough, this, so much so that Queen Mary was seen to look the other way, quite covered with something approaching confusion. In those days even the Wimbledon girls wore white stockings because Queen Mary hated bare legs.

NATIONAL SERVICE
The WI, quite properly, had serious matters to attend to. Norfolk Federation had its resolution supporting National Savings passed at the AGM. Every village, they said, should be given the opportunity to establish a branch. Today, hundreds of WIs have

savings groups and the NFWI is represented on the Executive Committee of the National Savings Committee. But the vital seed was sown way back in 1926.

SCHOOL LUNCHES
The WI pressed for 'adequate arrangements for school lunches' and Kelmscott, Oxfordshire, branch moved an AGM resolution to that effect. Indeed, the NFWI has battled on behalf of school meals and milk for many years. The campaign reached its height in 1937 when all WIs were urged to lobby their MPs to support the case for cheaper milk for mothers and children. Lady Denman herself went to the Commons and addressed groups of Members on this theme. But, alas, the reforms for which the WI had been pressing were only introduced during the last war.

They were also concerned about the health of the rural child which — so an Executive Committee resolution declared — had not kept pace with that of the urban child. The chief medical officer of the Board of Education suggested the WI could be of practical help.

CARE OF TEETH
Rothley WI in Northumberland moved a resolution welcoming an offer of the Dental Board to provide speakers for WI meetings on the care of teeth. In many homes, said the Rothley women, 'scant attention was paid to the state of children's teeth'.

National Health and other forms of insurance were also very much in their minds. Westmorland Federation urged all the WIs to study these problems. All the themes they supported or advocated in that year have borne fruit.

RURAL TELEPHONES
Even in 1927, when the infant telephone system was still settling down, the WI was doing its best to ginger up the rural service. An East Suffolk resolution urged a 'considerable reduction' in the amount required to be guaranteed in establishing a rural exchange and suggested that the overall profitability of the telephone service should be considered rather than the earning of individual exchanges.

The Federation also pressed for an all-night service. A system that shut down at 7.00 pm, particularly in isolated districts clearly had hazardous implications, especially in the case of fire and sickness.

The movement took rural telephones very seriously indeed.

Local MPs were lobbied by WIs and in 1928 the NFWI called together a representative meeting of MPs which elected a deputation to the postmaster general. The campaign was successful. The regulations affecting village telephones were amended and the guarantee position was eased.

Over the years there was a slow but steady increase in the numbers of village kiosks. The Federation was also successful in having heavy rentals removed from subscribers living more than three miles from an exchange and in securing a uniform rental system.

OIL POLLUTION

One of the most interesting of the early mandates concerned oil pollution. Appropriately, the first resolution on this theme came from the Isle of Wight in 1927. WIs all over the country were asked to take the matter seriously and to urge the government, 'without delay', to take all necessary steps to stop the further pollution of our seas and shores and to remove 'the terrible menace to the life both of our sea birds and fish'. In many social and environmental matters the WI has often been years ahead of its time.

ANTI-LITTER

For example, their first anti-litter resolution — a campaign which was to blossom into Keep Britain Tidy — was passed in 1925 and moved by Westmorland Federation. Here again the women felt they could play a particularly useful part by encouraging schools to train children in the matter.

As countrywomen, WI members have always sought to protect the countryside from the more dreadful incursions of 'towns'. In 1927 Northumberland Federation urged all the WIs to bring maximum pressure to bear on the county councils to enforce the by-laws to check 'the growing disfigurement of the countryside'.

Resolutions such as these stamped the NFWI as a national movement that really cared for Britain — a movement, moreover, not allied to any political end but rather a commonsense collection of average people who had views and ideas on and about the basic day-to-day conditions in a rapidly changing nation.

Campaigns and jubilees

medicines. It was always the town that profited from such action. To flush the system all the way down to the country involved a tremendous, unending fight. After all, in political terms, the country vote seemed less important. And it was a great deal more difficult to assess the conditions of the countryside from the insulated seat of government.

The flapper vote of 1928 extended the franchise to women of 21 and over, to bring it in line with male voters. That, too, extended the voice of the WI. But their members gained little from other so-called city delights of those years. The flapper herself was a town creature who visited the country with trepidation. The 'bright young things' of Noel Coward and Evelyn Waugh were rarely seen outside well-established mansions and hotels. The cocktail parties, the jazz, the increase in divorce, the Americanization of English culture, the mass consumer goods of Woolworths, the popularity of soccer and the cinema – these were primarily city pleasures.

Townspeople seeking to escape at weekends – the mass of 1930s' hikers and ramblers (more fashionable than walking) who set off in shorts happily along the country lanes and across the fields – expected to find a world of healthy, peaceful rustics. They anticipated a few brambles, exciting to break through, a little like Wimbledon Common, but on the whole they envisaged a countryside consisting of a well-ordered combination of meadow and copse, rather like Richmond or Hampstead, but hopefully provided with villages and farms which would welcome and revive them after the ardours of worthy exploration. There was a feeling among city people, not so dissimilar to that of today, that the towns would be taken care of by government and council – country folk should look after the rest.

A history of intolerance

So country folk spoke their mind, determined, in spite of everything, to make their villages worth living in as well as visiting. They wished to share in the 20th century and their earliest resolutions concerned new housing in the villages. Lloyd George had talked, at the end of the war, of 'homes fit for heroes'. They

WI fashions at the Annual General Meeting in London, 1922. Hats were a special feature in those days.

wanted homes fit to live in, that was all.

They were concerned about film censorship, the nature of crime-reporting in the press, the punishment of criminals, road safety; they wanted more adult education, VD posters, telephones in country districts, rural libraries; they wanted to see women do jury service, women police, instruction for women in rural life; they demanded better health care for their children, higher standards for bread, milk and honey, better conditions for nurses; they were indignant about oil pollution, performing animals, the exploitation of bird plumage, the disfigurement of rural scenery with advertisement hoardings.

It was work that never stopped. On their 21st birthday, Lady Denman asked, 'Are we satisfied that the beauty and value of our land is being preserved? Are we content with conditions of life in the countryside? Are we satisfied that our health services are adequate to our needs; or can ill-health and the disability which exists among women be lessened?'

If not satisfied, there were the words of Richard Crossman to spur them on. 'Do not underestimate how sensitive politicians are to a good nag,' he said at their Golden Jubilee. The worth of the WI, he said, was that they were determined to get things done; to do things as a group for themselves and, if they could not do it, to nag until it got done.'

'The history of the movement is one of *intolerance*,' exclaimed chairman Lady Brunner, teasing a WI resolution that emphasized the four spiritual values on which the movement was based: those of Fellowship, Truth, Justice and Tolerance. '*Intolerance* of burst pipes, children's horror comics, squalid newspapers and sordid litter. So long as there is cruelty or evil to harm children and young people,' she said; 'as long as animals are ill-treated; as long as there are ill-designed, shoddy goods on the market; as long as there is avoidable danger and hazard for young and old, whether on the roads, or by accidents in the home, or by food poisoning; as long as country people are badly in need of amenities they should share with townspeople – and as long as we are bound by fellowship, truth and justice, we can afford to be intolerant about a lot of things.'

Tireless energy

All this activity generated by the WI helped it grow through those difficult years. In 1927, there were already 250,000 happy and intolerant members in nearly 4,000 village WIs. By 1938 and the brink of a second war, the number had risen to 350,000 in five and a half thousand village WIs. As early as 1921, a 'mere man' reported that, 'If the Institute had done no more than to improve your village life, it would still have accomplished a great work.' He saw 'organizers with tireless energy penetrate to every village, lecturing, explaining and establishing women's institutes that can be social, intellectual and industrial centres of every community'.

There were some who saw this work in a different light. 'What is the use of women's institutes?' whined one early columnist. 'They revel in scandal and gossip and most of the demonstrations and lectures they have are far too complicated or take up too much time.' The National Federation knew that some WIs were weaker than others but Mr St John Ervine

replied on their behalf in an address to one village WI. 'My test of an educated person,' he said, 'is one who is not deceived by his paper.' And if the columnist regarded the activities of the WI as nothing better than interference in the community or the raising of their voices in complaint as a matter of mere clamour, *The Times* took another view altogether in 1924. 'The National Federation of Women's Institutes,' said that paper, 'is one of those comparatively rare democratic bodies which do a large amount of useful work and say very little about it.'

Three years later, in the *Manchester Guardian*, Mrs H. A. L. Fisher took a similar sensible and straightforward view. 'They are unobtrusive and infinitely important,' she wrote about the WI in an article on change in the villages, 'and when we come to reckon up all that has happened in the last ten years they play a considerable part. They give us among other things a common meeting ground, something to look forward to, and plenty to do, all remarkably good things.'

That was on the tenth birthday of the National Federation. In an article in *Queen* magazine that year, Mrs Watt appeared in print: 'So many of our results are intangible, so many are indirect, can never be measured,' she wrote. But, 'the Women's Institute has brought us all together, a happy working union of women of all sects, of all ages, of all grades of society, of varying capacity, at all stages of education and mental growth, of all politics, each with her own viewpoint and each with a personality which she is encouraged to develop. Somehow by the grace of self-control and tolerance, we have got a large measure of unity, mutual help and co-operation.'

The *Daily News* had already referred to the annual general meeting as 'the woman's parliament'. Now the *Southern Daily Echo* pronounced that 'to a certain extent the WIs have revolutionized rural life by awakening a spirit of corporate comradeship, practical endeavour and idealism which had for only too long lain latent among women of the countryside'. 'They definitely make life in the country districts happier, more hopeful and more useful than it could be without them. . . . The movement of these Women's Institutes has lighted a candle in England which will not

Campaigns and jubilees

easily be put out,' said *The Times*, for once a little carried away. It was a moment for pride.

The press continued to see the WI as 'campaigners, crusaders, relentless advocates for the betterment of life in the villages' but it was *The Times*, with a restored sense of equilibrium, which gave a balanced view of the developing picture of WI activity. Looking back on twenty years of bustle, the paper felt that 'it is not too much to say that there has never before been a woman's organization of such scope, durability and power' and, in explanation of this praise, selected 'the good and wise leadership', the care with which proposals were sifted until only the most reasonable became resolutions, the practical work such as marketing and the study of social laws; 'but it would be shooting very wide of the mark to suppose that all the annual programme was as serious as this', concluded the article. 'A great source of vitality is the amount of laughter, entertainment and happy activity.'

War and peace

There was indeed plenty of laughter and entertainment. There was a Handicraft Exhibition in the Victoria and Albert Museum as early as 1922. There was a National Drama Festival six years later and another at the end of the Great Depression. Queen Mary herself became a member and great interest was shown by the royal family. King George V's first Christmas Day broadcast in 1932 was heard by thousands of WI members just as it was by millions throughout the world. When his Silver Jubilee was loudly celebrated three years later and he was heard to murmur, as he drove through cheering London, 'I'd no idea they felt like that about me', no doubt the WI was keen to cheer with all the others.

It celebrated its 21st birthday alongside the coronation of King George VI and Queen Elizabeth and presented Lady Denman with a book made up of pages representing aspects of every county. 'I can truthfully say that nothing that has ever been given to me has given me so much pleasure,' she wrote to Mrs Munro, who had supervised the production of the book, 'not only from the sentimental point of view

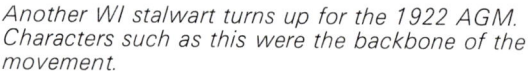
Another WI stalwart turns up for the 1922 AGM. Characters such as this were the backbone of the movement.

but also because of the real charm of the book.'

Then the WI was thrown into the confusion of another war. Once more they turned to the land to replenish the nation's dwindling larder. They did much more. In 1940, they received a message from the Queen, who praised their 'important National Service . . . including work for evacuees, co-operative work on comforts for men of the Services, and hospital supplies; also co-operative buying of vegetable and potato seeds to increase our food supply'. At the same time, they planned busily for peace and published pamphlets to map out the future. They studied the spate of reports on social welfare which appeared during the war, they filled in government questionnaires on agricultural wages and bad housing, and they gave evidence on deprived children.

As always agriculture was revitalized by the

Trapped! HRH the Duke of Edinburgh meets the WI in the mass at the WI's Golden Jubilee Royal Garden Party at Buckingham Palace in 1965.

war. County War Agricultural Committees were set up to distribute subsidies and encourage mechanization and the use of fertilizers. Mechanical horse-power on the farms rose from two to five million during the war years. There were accusations that farmers were 'feather-bedded' but there was much lost ground to be made up. Five million acres were turned over to tillage and fertilizers increased the yield per acre. Only dairy cattle increased in number; other stock declined.

The number of WI members also declined during the first few years of war. They dropped from 331,000 in 1940 to a low of 288,000 in 1943, as many busied themselves with other work. As the war drew to a close they revived and by 1945 there were over 300,000 members again. In 1947, Stoney Creek celebrated its Golden Jubilee – a reminder of happier times.

The WI had their own end-of-war celebrations. They prepared for their first Combined Arts Festival and laid plans for their own adult education college. Denman College was opened in 1948, the biggest project the WI had ever undertaken. Simultaneously they faced the post-war crisis with a renewed burst of food production. Operation Produce carried on the wartime traditions.

Changing faces

The post-war period was one of changing faces. Lady Denman retired in 1946, after thirty years as chairman. The Queen said to her fellow members, 'She has led us with a just sense of proportion and balance, with the humour that is so essential to a chairman, and she has the quality which a leader must have, that of being able to go on learning and keeping up with the changing times. I suppose that Lady Denman's contribution towards the happiness and progress of rural life is one of the greatest that has been made in our time. I hope she realizes the deep gratitude and affection which members feel for her.' Lady Denman died at home eight years later, on the day of the annual general meeting. The news was kept from delegates until they left the Albert Hall.

By the time Lady Denman resigned, the Honourable Frances Farrer was over half-way through her own period of thirty years as General Secretary. She had succeeded Inez Jenkins in 1929. Awarded the DBE in 1950, Dame Frances worked in the WI headquarters in Eccleston Street, London, for so long that it seemed the building was her own, dominated by her precise memory and her special interest in public questions. She is remembered with affection as something of a martinet who loved her work and stuck up for the village WI and County secretaries. Lady Dyer remembers Dame Frances meeting one of the secretaries one day, putting her arm round her and saying, 'We must have lots to talk about'. And she meant it.

Now Dame Frances lives in a house in Abinger Hammer, Surrey, once rented from her family by E. M. Forster, where she receives many visitors, including groups of enthusiastic Japanese, who come to pay homage to the home of the novelist. She has more time to devote to the welfare of her own village than she did in her London days and does so with deep interest and considerable energy of mind.

In the thirty-odd years since Lady Denman's own spell of 30 years, there have been seven chairmen of the WI. Her successor, Lady Albemarle, proposed a five-year limit for chairmen. 'If you can't make it in five years,' she says, 'you won't make it at all. If you haven't already, then you won't anyway; if you have, then you'll have used up all your ideas.'

Her husband called Lady Albemarle a 'civil servant manqué' and others who knew her well have described how active and effective she was on the national executive of the WI. Her main concern was that the WI should work in the changing post-war world to resist bad change and encourage the good. She confesses that she only learnt Italian and needlework through the WI but she was also chairman of the Development Commission, a member of the Arts Council and, in 1949, the only woman member of the British delegation to the UNESCO Conference in Copenhagen. Like Lady Denman, she was very good at dealing with government ministers.

The creation of Denman College was partly her work and partly that of her successor, Lady Brunner, a woman of legendary warmth, whose theatrical background – her grandfather was Sir Henry Irving and she had acted at the Royal Court – was a positive advantage at big meetings. 'It gave her timing,' says her husband, 'and taught her to use her hands.' 'As Macmillan said in one of those interviews,' adds Lady Brunner, 'you must never make a weak gesture from the elbow.'

A balanced meal

'I can't think how you would live in a village if you didn't belong to the WI,' says Lady Brunner; 'it would be like eating bread and milk instead of a good balanced meal.' Despite her interest in Denman College and the educational side of the WI, Lady Brunner, like many others, was quick to recognize the importance of that sense of balance. 'The WI is like a white post,' she adds; 'it is subject to a torrent of change. To keep it white you need coats and coats of paint.'

There *were* coats of paint. There were festivals and jubilees whenever possible. All were marked by the high standards that have been such an important aspect of WI work and play. Lady Albemarle presided over the first Singing Festival and the celebrations for the Festival of Britain in 1951. Lady Brunner presided over the formation of the Keep Britain Tidy Group. Her successor, Lady Dyer, presided over another Drama Festival, WI contributions to World Refugee Year, and a Country Feasts and Festivals Competition.

Lady Dyer was persuaded to join the WI by her cook, who saw it as a good way to get a lift for herself to the meeting. She continued to take a special interest in the ordinary members and, as chairman, was determined to create a feeling of trust between local and national

Lady Albermarle, as Chairman, addressing delegates at The Annual General Meeting in the Albert Hall.

levels and to make it easier for the village WIs to understand what the resolutions at the Albert Hall were all about. She did not want the villagers to be forced into doing things beyond their comprehension. At the same time, she felt, like Lady Denman, that it was important that the WI pushed a little beyond the caring of the ordinary person. Once again, it was a question of balance. It was also a question of stamina. Lady Dyer knew every county chairman and was reputed to bike fourteen miles each way to committees during the war.

Enjoying the Jubilee Year

The next chairman had an even better memory for faces, as well she needed to when she walked with the Queen in the gardens of Buckingham Palace amongst 9,000 country women on the occasion of the WI Golden Jubilee in 1965. Mrs Gabrielle Pike also paid an official visit to the Soviet Union on behalf of the WI. She presided over the first National Art Exhibition, the raising of £182,000 among the village WIs in aid of the Freedom From Hunger Campaign, and the rescinding of the '4,000 Rule' – the rule by which the formation of WIs had been limited to places with populations under 4,000. She was also the first untitled chairman of the WI.

'Let's enjoy the Jubilee Year,' she said in her message to the WI in *Home and Country*, 'and

have some fun.' Never averse to that aspect of their lives, members listened eagerly as Mrs Pike continued: 'Let's enjoy the picnics, the barbecues, the bonfires, the pageants and the parties. Let it be a memorable year, one we will never forget, and one which will be the beginning of a new chapter in our lives.' The members heartily agreed.

Cornwall set the pace by arranging a special train to take their representatives up to London for the royal garden party. The 'Cornish Train' has become part of the folklore of the WI. There was a special dining car for WI teas and a coach reserved for changing. The junketings at the Palace on May 31, 1965, were supposed to begin at three o'clock and continue until six but the enthusiastic members – a representative from every village WI – arrived with resolute earliness and remained steadfastly till late. The Palace, according to Mrs Pike, hardly knew what had hit it.

Food was provided by Lyons but it was overdainty food, unfit for hungry country appetites, and it disappeared within five minutes. Lyons calmly replaced it. Equal calmness was shown by the woman down from Norfolk found changing behind a sentry box. 'You don't think, do you, that I'm going to meet the Queen in *this* dress?' she said.

'They had such *fun*,' remembers Mrs Pike. 'I don't remember a cross word throughout that period.' It took the Queen and herself three hours to walk down the lawn through the crowd. She apologized for the crush. The Queen replied that she remembered a time when her parents had given a party for 8,000 after the war. The crush was so great that the royal party had slipped out of one gate, walked down Buckingham Palace Road unobserved and back through a side entrance.

This day of justifiable celebration was a nice balance to the more serious side of WI work. Only the year before Mrs Pike had talked of the 'vast untapped collective energy of the institutes' and asked them what they were going to do next. She herself had been brought up by her father to see the WI as a 'mission', a way of life. She is descended from Elizabeth Fry, the famous prison reformer, and her father was the bishop of Lichfield, who used to stroll around his parishioners garbed in the bishop's mauve top and a pair of shorts. Mrs

Pike set a fine example to the WI by being the only woman appointed to a committee of five set up to enquire into the Aberdeen typhoid outbreak of 1964. She continues to sit on many committees.

The greatest praise she remembers, however, was received in a letter from Dame Frances Farrer, who said that when she heard her speak at the AGM, it was 'just like Trudy Denman all over again'. No one was ever slow to appreciate inspiring leadership.

Putting their house in order

In 1966, while Mrs Pike congratulated the WI on enjoying themselves so much the previous year, during their Jubilee celebrations, the members got to grips with their financial problems. Mrs Jacob – now chairman of the WI – set them the task of raising half a million pounds to 'save the National Federation'. Mrs Pike had wanted to make it a million but that was thought too ambitious. Within two years of the new fund-raising effort, half the amount had been accumulated by the village WIs, employing every conceivable method, barring the illegal, to obtain that extra £10 here or £5 there. The Appeal was finally closed over the half million mark – a magnificent response by WI members.

In the year of the launching of the Appeal, Lady Anglesey became chairman. Anglesey had, of course, been the home of the first WI in Britain. The new chairman was the daughter of Charles Morgan, the novelist, and she herself had grown up in Wales and took a special interest in Welsh members, encouraging bilingual meetings to enrich community spirit.

With the rise in nationalist feelings, many Welsh members felt a long way from National Federation headquarters in London. Some wanted meetings to be held only in Welsh. These members were attracted by an alternative organization called the Mercherd Y Wawr, or Daughters of the Dawn. To keep the WI intact, the National Federation has made great efforts to remind Welsh members that they are not only an integral part of the WI but actually represent the origins of the WI in Britain and fully reflect its aims.

The Freedom From Hunger Campaign was still in progress during Lady Anglesey's chairmanship and she toured Colombia and the Caribbean to see how WI money was being spent. Her main interests were in the environment and the arts. She sat on the Royal Commission on the Environment and is chairman of the Welsh Arts Council. She organized the 1963 WI National Art Exhibition and she presided over the specially commissioned operatic sequence, 'The Brilliant and the Dark', performed by the WI in the Albert Hall in 1969.

Lady Anglesey also put forward the proposal for Full Free Family Planning. She believes that membership of the WI can lead to 'a great deal that one has done in one's life outside the family and also a lot that's gone on inside the family'. Family Planning was one family matter on which she found evidence of a considerable change in attitude.

A change of outlook

It was because of this changing attitude and the eagerness of many WI members to discuss all matters that concerned them closely that the next chairman, Miss Sylvia Gray, presided over a fundamental change in the Constitution of the WI. This change concerned the interpretation of the non-party political, non-sectarian rule, which had been the subject of heated argument ever since the WI first began.

As we have seen, the rule enabled members to sink their differences and ensure that no discussion hurt anyone's feelings or beliefs. Without that rule, the WI would have lost a great deal of its original reason for being. What *is* important to understand, of course, is that membership of the WI did not stop anyone from joining any other organization they wished. In fact, it was made easier for them to join more partisan organizations because whatever they joined did not prejudice their WI membership. They could belong to church or chapel, the Mothers' Union, the Labour, Liberal, Conservative or Communist Parties but at WI meetings they left individual beliefs outside the door.

Institute membership was essentially something *extra* to life. For some, it might occupy

Lady Albemarle, 1946–1951.

Lady Brunner, 1951–1956.

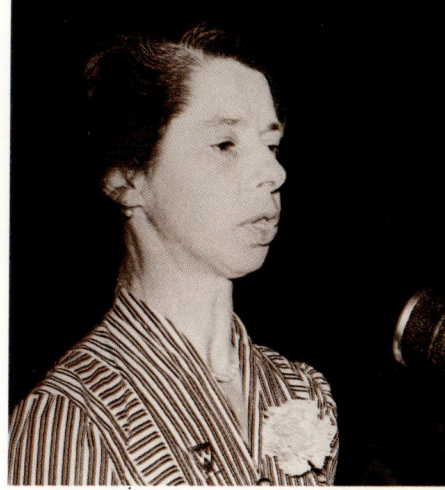

Lady Dyer, 1956–1961.

Mrs Gabrielle Pike, 1961–1966.

There have been six national chairmen since Lady Denman retired in 1946.

Lady Anglesey, 1966–1969.

Miss Sylvia Gray, 1969–1974.

most of their time; for others it might be one of many interests. But everyone knew, whatever they did or believed, there was one place they could meet without friction, enjoy themselves together and discuss common problems.

One other factor may have contributed a little to the importance laid by the WI on this rule: a reaction to the treatment of conscientious objectors during the First World War. Their imprisonment and the attitudes taken by both press and public were seen by many as a dangerous erosion of individual freedom of expression and belief, producing, as did the horror of war itself, a sense of moral debasement. It was in defence of these freedoms that the rule was so strictly maintained.

Lady Brunner saw the rule as the rock on which the WI rested. She praised the 'vigilance of those in responsible positions and the wisdom that was brought to founding our Constitution . . . Had we not stuck to our stern conception of being non-party political and non-sectarian we might well have foundered', she said, 'for we have grown to maturity in a

51

Campaigns and jubilees

world full of conflict – where suspicion and mistrust have too often resulted from the stresses and hardships of past decades – where sympathy and understanding too often are still-born because of prejudice or jealousy. We may be criticized from time to time by all political parties and religious bodies but we can be content to be a common meeting ground which can also be a stepping stone to a variety of wider and deeper experiences.'

Criticized they were, from the beginning. In 1923, the *Manchester Guardian* warned against the dangers inherent in the non-party rule: 'Political acrimony might be a real danger to their (the WIs') well-being but it could hardly be as dangerous as intellectual lethargy.' There was truth in the comment and *Home and Country* replied in an article the following year: 'Citizens of a state cannot have too much knowledge of civic affairs nor can they take too intelligent an interest in the methods of governing their country. . . . The institutes must keep out party but may open the door wide to politics.'

The *Dorset Chronicle* agreed wholeheartedly that this was a good thing: 'The extraordinary progress of the Women's Institutes movement in the county of Dorset, as elsewhere, has been largely due to the fact that they have supplied a pleasant rallying ground in which social distinctions are to a large extent obliterated and from which sectarian and political controversies are rigidly excluded.'

In 1942, *Home and Country* returned to the subject and reminded readers that they could work through their churches individually if they wished. The article quoted Grace Hadow's views of 1929 on the subject of religion: 'It is a natural desire on the part of those who feel most keenly that their Institute fellowship is the outcome of their religious convictions to express their faith in words, but speech is not the only form of self-expression. "Actions speak louder than words" and the faith expressed by the comradeship of a Women's Institute surely ranks with that which reveals itself in uttered prayer.'

The war years brought particular criticism of the WI, for many people expected it to contribute by civil defence work to the national war effort. Sticking to its rule and in deference to its Quaker members, the WI remained pacifist, though contributing substantially to the war effort by helping with such schemes as the evacuation programme and the fruit-preserving programme. Members helped individually, of course, as they wished, either in civil or military defence. Numbers declined sharply at the beginning of the war but picked up in time as people recognized the sense of continuity that the WI offered. Confidence grew as people saw the work it was doing and the plans it was making for peace. A spirit of common sense was maintained and the Institutes were a way in which those working hard at their own war-work could relax together for a time or contribute to some other communal effort.

By the 1970s, some modification of the rule seemed essential to allow members greater freedom of discussion. Facing the future, Sylvia Gray warned that the conference called to discuss changes to the Constitution was 'bound to be controversial and it's going to be difficult but there will soon be a very different generation of members and we must take a very hard look at these questions. It ought to be stimulating and rewarding if we tackle it with tolerance and a sense of humour.'

There was, in fact, only a small addition proposed to the old rule. 'The character of the movement is non-sectarian and non-party political . . .' ran the familiar words, 'but,' came the addition, 'this shall not be interpreted so as to prevent Women's Institutes from concerning themselves with matters of political or religious significance, provided the views and rights of minorities are respected and provided the movement is never used for party-political or sectarian propaganda.'

WIs were divided in their reaction. One felt that 'We must move from being an organization of the early 20th century to being a movement of the *late* 20th century.' Another feared that 'partisan groups might use the WI movement'. One asked, 'Would the government listen to us if it knew we were open to pressure from various factions?' Another expressed the more homely but nonetheless important fear that on many subjects there would inevitably be disagreement, 'and we all wish to remain friends'.

In response, Lady Albemarle asked, 'Why have we been educating ourselves for over fifty years if we cannot now tackle more difficult problems?' Government, she said, was intruding further and further into their lives; they *must* discuss what it was doing or they would not be able to continue to serve the useful purposes they had hitherto been doing; they would certainly lose the leaders of their movement and they might well put off potential members. Finally, she thought that many WIs were already, of their own accord, doing what the new resolution suggested. 'It is a change we must have the courage to make,' she said; 'we must cease to break the rules.' She concluded by quoting Lady Denman, who was accustomed to comment in times of stress, 'Trust the Institutes'.

The trust proved well-founded, as Miss Gray remembers. 'The time seemed just right to rely on the common sense of the members not to allow themselves to be used for party political purposes,' she said and she considers that the new rule was the most important thing that happened during her term of office as national chairman. Of course, problems still arose over religious discussion, as when a County officer was introduced to her local WI by the president. 'This evening one of our crosses comes to life,' she said, referring to the x-mark by which the officer had been elected on the ballot paper. But there were several red faces.

Passionate for moderation

Miss Gray was involved with many things. She helped to launch a Music Society for the WI and a tennis tournament. She obtained a grant for a Town and Country Project to look into the relationship between the two. She initiated a public relations post in the WI. She was the first chairman of the WI who was also a professional woman and has run a hotel in the Cotswolds since 1935 which has an all-female staff and to which girls come to train for hotel management. Miss Gray's interests extend to the National Consumer Council, the Post Office Users Council, the National Trust and local government. Although she thinks it important to return to the simple pleasures of the past at village and county level, she has found, paradoxically, that it was the older members rather than the younger ones who

The present chairman, Alderman Mrs Pat Jacob, JP, took over in 1974. She faces difficult economic problems in a time of high inflation.

were more in favour of the constitutional changes over which she presided.

The present chairman took over in 1974. Alderman Pat Jacob faces the problems of an increasingly urbanized membership, as the distinction at the edges of town and country blur. Both town and country face the same bureaucratic tedium of modern living problems. One bright diamond – a Diamond Jubilee – has already brought a sparkle to her term of office. It was Lady Anglesey who summed up WI achievements in 1975, their Diamond Year:

'For sixty years we have been outspoken but also moderate; today the pressures are stronger to act emotionally and sectionally and to move towards extremes. These pressures will be on us too. Tolerant and informed we must continue to be, apathetic we must not become, but our spread, geographically and socially through a considerable cross-section of society, gives us a special opportunity – to be passionate for moderation, to hang on to rational argument and common sense, and to work for the good of the whole community. It will require strenuous activity and may not be at all easy. Let us make sure that by the time we reach our centenary our members still enjoy the same opportunity for freedom of expression.'

The challenge of war

LIKE the nation, the WI faced its greatest challenge in the war. In 1939, members resolved their monthly meetings should remain islands of common sense, tranquility and cheerfulness in a sadly troubled world. Tranquility they needed, for their first job proved a nightmare. Days before the declaration of war on Sunday, September 3, the evacuees began to arrive from London.

They had nearly come the year before, as Spelsbury WI recalled: 'thousands of school children, busloads of unaccompanied babies, threatening startled and unprepared villages with only two days warning but cancelled almost as soon as they were announced. It was the babies that made the villages of Oxfordshire so particularly thankful when "Munich" occurred. Now, a year later, it had all been properly organized. There was to be no wild, general stampede from the fear of bombs such as had been expected the year before. For four days almost the only trains that left London were those carrying school children, mothers with children under five, expectant mothers (with special pink labels attached), the blind, the crippled and the inmates of Poor Law Infirmaries.'

Preparations were made in the villages for the invasion, accommodation found, spare houses cleared out, beds made but, like all good plans, even these were subject to radical revision at the last moment. Spelsbury waited with other villages at the station to greet an expected 900 school children and was confronted, instead, with 900 mothers and babies.

Hospitable as the villagers tried and intended to be, friction soon developed. Strange children in the house were one thing; adults with firmly entrenched habits quite another. *The Times* boasted of the brilliant organization that had evacuated smoothly three million people out of the capital but nothing was said of the inevitable cultural clash that followed.

Those who remember with nostalgia 'sober little figures, brothers and sisters keeping close together; all with those terribly unmanageable gas-mask boxes dangling like lockets round their necks or bumping against their hips, with their luggage in brown-paper carriers, and "twopenny" comics rolled up under their arms' might read with profit the report that the WI produced on their experience. It is called 'Town Children Through Country Eyes'.

The report does not set out to condemn those children or their mothers but rather the town system that produced them. Plenty of children settled down happily enough once they got used to the countryside but mothers who could not settle returned to the town. The WI acknowledged the sense of dislocation felt both by mothers and children but recounted the facts as they appeared to long-suffering country wives coping with indignant city mothers cajoled into the country by promises of comfort and safety they could not recognize.

The facts were lice and scabies, bed-wetting, total lack of hygiene or mother-care. 'In practically every batch of children there were some who suffered from head-lice, skin diseases and bed-wetting,' said the report, to which one father replied, 'All children breed head lice and it couldn't be helped.' Some children 'never actually used a lavatory; the children simply sat down in the house anywhere to relieve themselves and actually one woman who, was given the guest room . . . always sat the baby in the bed for this purpose . . . When soiled beyond possible use under-blankets were just flung into cupboards instead of being washed.' One mother was seen to wrap her child's wetted pants around the teapot to dry them.

As for diet, 'the children are used to being

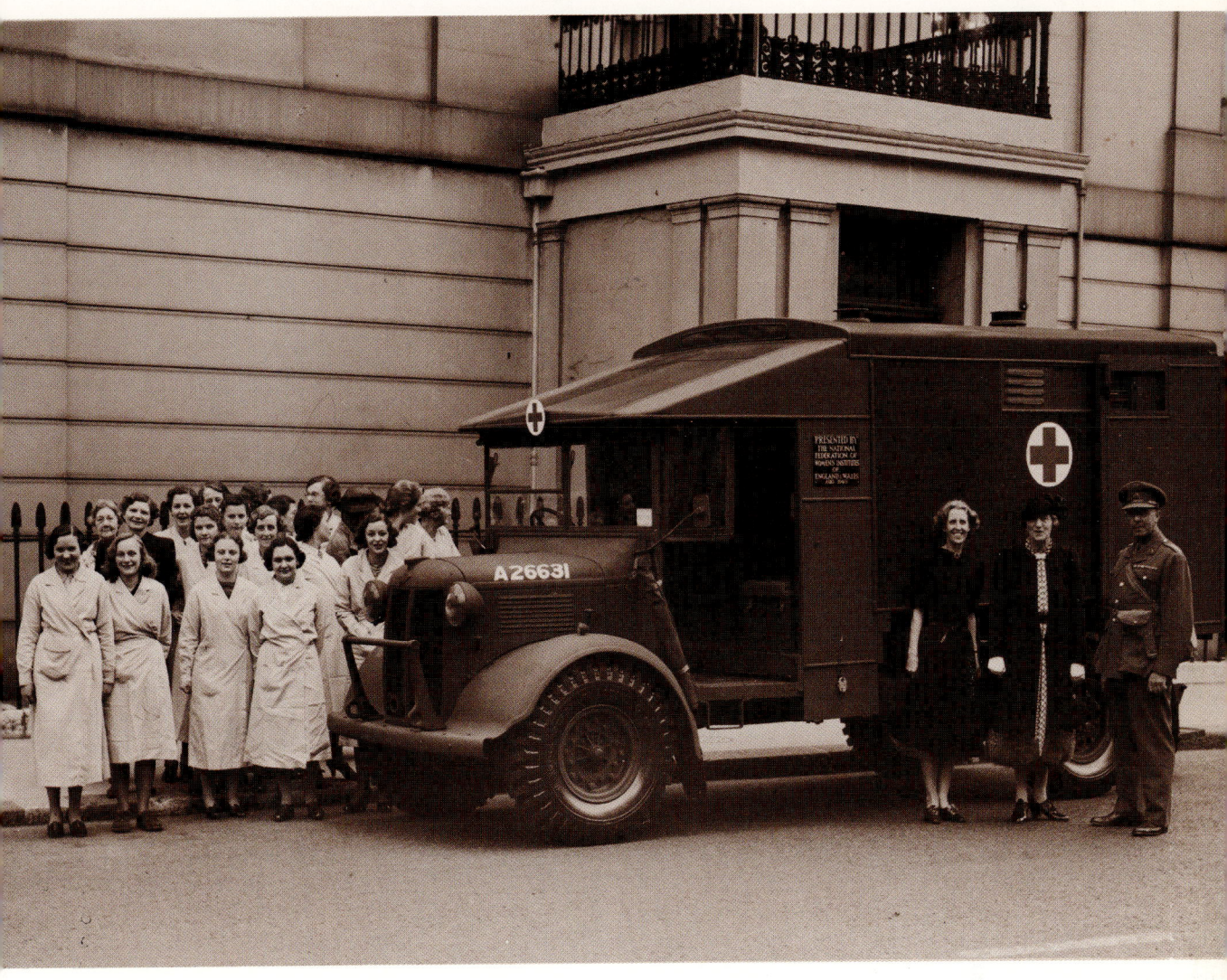

fed on "pieces" (bread and margarine), fish and chips, tinned food and sweets'. 'Vegetables (other than potatoes) and puddings were unknown to many children.' 'Some said they had never seen their mother cook anything and had no hot meals at home.' The same story is repeated over and over again: the two boys who attempted to eat soup with a knife and fork, because they had never had any before; the little girl of five and a half who said she would like her usual beer and cheese for supper; the mother who said her child was not getting enough fresh fruit (oranges and bananas) when there were plenty of apples and plums to be had for the picking up, if she'd wanted.

Of course there were the amusing stories, to be associated with any town-dweller confront-

Dame Frances Farrer, left, a former WI General Secretary, with Lady Denman outside the WI's London HQ, with the ambulance which the WI presented to the Army in 1940.

ing the oddities of the countryside. There were the complaints against 'dirty' vegetables; there was amazement at the sight of fruit growing on trees and the realization that hens laid eggs and cows gave milk. Newspapers were full of stories and cartoons: 'Mummy, its called spring; they have one every year.' But there were also the children who had never in their life slept in a bed. They needed clothes but only comics and sweets arrived from their parents or, if clothes came, often they had to be burnt at once because of their condition.

These were children from the slums, under-nourished, dumped unceremoniously in a

The challenge of war

strange world. There were plenty of others who were happy and healthy. Even the slum children, fed, cleaned and made fit again by practical country housewives, began to respond and enjoy themselves. One little boy in Chidham soon was heard singing as he washed himself. His song was about 'Old Itler'. 'Hitler,' said his hostess but the boy knew his own mind. 'It 'ain't worth soundin' an 'aitch for 'im,' he said.

The suburban or slum housewife, confronted by an earth privy, no electricity, no cinema and few neighbours, might be forgiven for reacting with bitterness but such bitterness could not explain the ruined beds that villagers were forced to burn after their departure, the broken toys and furniture, the sense of outrage in the villages. Their report opened the closed eyes of the authorities.

'It would be difficult to overstate the value of this survey,' said one authority, 'so obviously unbiased and full of acute observations. I feel that, subject to any possible over-riding considerations it should be given the widest publicity.' Copies were sent to Health and Education officials in urban areas from which the children had come. The minister of health sent a note of appreciation. 'The WIs have earned the warm thanks of the government and the gratitude of the mothers of Britain,' he wrote. 'They have taken their guests into the life of the countryside, worked in the sweat of their brows on community tasks, and made the city "at home" by the village firesides. This was vital to the success of the evacuation scheme.'

He could say that again, about the sweat of their brows. At the end of the war, he did so. He said they had done 'one of the finest and hardest jobs of the war on the home front – 24 hours a day, seven days a week. Evacuation has saved many thousands of children from death or injury'.

The archbishop of Canterbury backed the minister's statement. 'Women's Institutes have been the means,' he said, 'of seeking out hitherto unexpected proofs of the resourcefulness, the capacity, the intelligence and the initiative of our country women. Everywhere they have been ready to put themselves at the disposal of the communities in which they live.' Indeed, their wholehearted involvement in this area was in itself a massive war effort.

Between 1940 and 1945 more than 5300 tons of fruit were preserved by the WI. Here we see the Fruit Preservation Centre at Thornton-le-Dale in Yorkshire in full swing.

Jam

The second major contribution that the WI made to the nation's war effort was a replay of their success in the First World War. They were invited by the Ministry of Agriculture to organize a Co-operative Fruit Preservation Scheme to save and make use of surplus fruit. *Home and Country* set the note of enthusiasm for the jam-makers of 1940 with the slogan, 'Produce – preserve: these are the watchwords of the Women's Institutes in these summer days of stress.' They gave away with their July issue a leaflet describing two ways of preserving fruit without sugar.

One month later, the minister of agriculture made a bulldog announcement: 'This war may well be decided by the last week's supply of food. It is up to all of us now to see that *our* people have that last week's supply.' The WI took the message by the throat. Within a month the number of jam and preservation centres shot up from 157 to 1855.

Five hundred Dixie Hand Sealers – or home-canners – came from America, with a complete large-scale Fruit Preservation Unit and oil stoves, preserving pans, tea-towels, thermometers, jam jars, bottling jars, jam pot covers and special discs for pickles and chutneys.

Armed with this equipment, the centres went to work in village halls, stables and farm kitchens, competing for space with farm animals, evacuees, quartered troops, the problems of air-raid precautions, first-aid classes, gas decontamination centres and a thousand other interferences of war.

At the end of 1940, 1631 tons of fruit had been preserved – that is over three and a half million pounds! Between 1940 and 1945, over 5300 tons had been saved, or very nearly twelve million pounds of fruit that might otherwise have been wasted. If reports came in of a glut of cherries on a nearby farm, it was no use to complain that notice was too short to pick that day. 'Absolute nonsense, get on with it,' was the order and on that particular day in Somerset 780 pounds were picked, jammed and canned on the spot.

Allocations of sugar were provided by the Ministry and strictly accounted for. Recipes had to be approved, canners had to possess a Certificate of Competence to Can issued by the National Federation, and spot checks were frequently made. This was unfortunate for the Somerset canners who had been using one of their tins for bits of waste paper and rubbish. Someone carelessly sealed the tin. The checker chose that tin to test!

All labour, by members as well as non-members, was free and *all* produce had to be sold back to the Ministry or the trade at agreed prices. Once rationing began, no helper was allowed to buy anything from her own centre – which was hard luck, when you had made good jam all day long. But it did discourage unfair handouts of extra food.

Miss Vera Cox, who organized the WI markets for many years, remembers some of the problems. In 1941 she reported in *Home and Country*: 'At one centre half the members cycled five miles before breakfast to pick the fruit, other members prepared and served them breakfast and the rest preserved the fruit in the afternoon. Letters tell of centres being taken over by the Military "as our jam was put on to boil". A secretary apologizes for her forms (a report on each centre) being late by saying, "My house was bombed and it was so difficult to find things afterwards." Another centre had their leader killed when her cottage was hit. Dog fights took place overhead but as one leader said, "You can't leave jam cooking and take shelter." The scheme may have been improvised,' concluded Miss Cox, 'but the work was done and the fruit was preserved, and through all the notes on the forms and the letters accompanying them runs the willingness to undertake a further scheme in 1941.'

Best known of all the tales of determination comes from the East Kent village of Hawkinge – a tale which cannot be left unrepeated. Evacuation from the risks of bombing had reduced membership of the local WI from more than a hundred to five women determined to stay on their land. Rejecting a County Federation offer to buy back from them the canner they had bought in their more prosperous days, they resolved to get on with the jam.

'We couldn't go away and do war work,' said one of the five, 'and we thought, well, we could do *that*.' So they took turns at stirring and taking shelter during air-raids. Even during the heaviest raids, the boiling jam was watched closely and in the worst raid of all the youngest stayed, determined to stir till the last. 'You see,' she said, 'the others had children and I have not.' By the end of the season, the five of them had made nearly 800 pounds of jam and filled another 800 cans and 100 bottles with preserves.

Less well-known is the story from Hyde Heath, in Buckinghamshire. The day after the Queen had paid a visit to their canning centre, Lord Haw Haw reported in his broadcast that the Queen had visited a 'cannon' factory. 'Not long afterwards,' writes a member, 'bombs were dropped near the railway line which runs right through our parish, and many of the houses had roof damage.' Hitler had lost his sweet tooth.

Jam jars occasionally ran short but an Oxfordshire WI had the answer. An expedition was made to London with car and trailer and WVS escort to raid the rubbish dumps of the capital, from which were gathered a great number of highly suitable containers. On such initiatives did the WI thrive.

Herbs
for medicines

The WI throve in a great variety of activities besides. Herb collecting was a valuable addi-

A memorable period. It began in 1928, the year in which the vote was extended to women of 21 – the culmination of years of campaigning. Our picture shows how women had been pressing for a vote since the end of the 19th century. From then the pace of change was to become ever more rapid and bewildering, with the Wall Street crash and massive unemployment. But the WI took time off from these great issues to campaign on behalf of performing animals.

If anyone doubts that history repeats itself a glance through the WI's mandates should put them right. Consider this 1929 resolution from the Worcestershire Federation:

HOME FOOD PRODUCTION

'Recognizing the growing importance of sidelines in agriculture, County Federations are urged to give practical assistance to WI members in the development of their own resources for home food production.'

The resolution also called attention to the 'urgent necessity' of promoting the development of fruit culture and preservation in England and Wales.

Time and again the Federation was to revert to this theme.

PERFORMING ANIMALS

The interests of members ranged over most of the current themes of the day. Performing animals were viewed with some concern by the Shropshire Federation. A national resolution of 1930 considered that the importing of performing animals into Great Britain should be stopped. Most of these animals, said the resolution, were trained in countries where no adequate cruelty prevention measures existed.

SEWING

The National Federation's Executive Committee put forward a resolution about sewing. Concerned about the standard of plain sewing as taught in rural elementary and secondary schools, the Executive urged all the WIs to approach their local authorities to see if the standard could be improved. WI members in those days had no doubts about the roles of the sexes. In 1936 Kemerton WI, Gloucestershire, put it quite bluntly: if children stayed at school until they were fifteen then, in the last two years of their school life, the girls should be instructed in domestic subjects and boys should receive special training depending on their future employment. Whatever the theorists of today might think, in 1936 this was an eminently sensible suggestion.

ANCIENT BUILDINGS

The late 1920s and early 30s saw a rapid increase in ribbon development and the face of Britain's high-streets also began to change. There was an urgent need to protect ancient buildings and the WI was in the forefront of the battle. In 1930 the Executive Committee urged WIs throughout the country to help preserve ancient buildings in their own areas.

Meanwhile, in national affairs these were significant years for women. In 1928 the vote was extended to all women of 21 and over. This was the famous 'votes for flappers' issue. The following year saw the first woman in a British cabinet – Margaret Bondfield, who was Minister of Labour in Ramsay MacDonald's government.

1929 was also the year of the Wall Street crash, which effectively shattered the monetary and credit system of the Western world. Unemployment shot up. In Germany the figure reached six million in 1932.

How much in key with world events was the WI during those vital years of the early thirties, when a frustrated Germany, fed up with trundling Reichsmarks to the bank in barrow loads and squirming beneath the sanctions imposed at Versailles, was turning to National Socialism and a new hero in the shape of Adolf Hitler?

Most national movements are rooted in the ethos of their age and country. The WI was no exception. The civilized, humanist instincts of the British were in fine fettle as several WI resolutions demonstrated. Politically and economically the year was a memorable one for Britain. The Labour government collapsed, we left the gold standard and there was a mutiny in the fleet over rumoured pay cuts. There were also more than three and a quarter million Britons unemployed.

DENMAN REPORT

The practical education of women for rural life lay at the very core of the movement. The first resolution urging action was passed in 1924 and in the following year Lady Denman was appointed Chairman of an Inter-departmental Committee whose terms of reference were 'To consider the practical education of women for life and to make recommendations'.

This report – which bears Lady Denman's name – was published in 1928 and after a long struggle by the movement to get the recommendations adopted, the Ministry of Agriculture announced its decision to recognize Rural Domestic Economy as a branch of adult education. In 1944 the Education Act of that year placed responsibility for further education on the local authorities.

And so the early Thirties limped along in a gathering cloud of uncertainty and unreality. One of the key figures of the time was Canon Dick Sheppard, a radio preacher of vast appeal, who founded the Peace Pledge Union in 1934. Within one year more than 80,000 people had pledged themselves on postcards not to fight in a war – and between ten

and eleven million people in the celebrated 'Peace Ballot' endorsed a reduction in armaments policy. The Peace Pledge Union even advocated the abolition of national military and naval aircraft. Britain, it seemed, was engulfed in its own massive internal crisis.

While footpath preservation, hire purchase regulations and the necessity for entirely natural and unadulterated honey were matters for WI consideration in the few years that lay ahead before disaster, other nations were solving their economic problems by far more militant means. But that is a later story.

DISARMAMENT

May, 1932. Gloucestershire Federation reflected the prevailing mood of the country in a resolution urging world disarmament.

It seemed so logical, sensible and sweetly reasonable at the time. Europe was in a state of economic depression. Why concentrate on guns — surely butter was far more important and in any equation between guns and butter most people in these islands had few doubts which to plump for: butter, every time.

UNEMPLOYMENT

The Executive Committee 'remembering that the NFWI was founded in a time of crisis to serve Home and Country', called upon all Women's Institutes through the country to support efforts in their own locality to deal with unemployment and distress among both men and women.

tion to their war work. Miss Cummings, a rural domestic economy instructress, who gained an MBE for her work in the war, mobilized the women of the countryside to utilize home-produced food to its fullest extent. She visited every small village in a wide area of southern England and organized the WIs into collecting parties to roam the Berkshire Hills. They searched for herbs and wild seeds in vast quantities for the manufacture of much-needed drugs.

The Berkshire Herb Committee reported in 1944 that 'Hips are urgently required this year for the manufacture of a Vitamin C syrup. The target for Berkshire is fifteen tons – nearly double the total for 1943.' Twopence per pound would be paid for the hips and it was warned that they should be picked on a dry day when turning from green to red. 'Foxglove seed is also wanted for the manufacture of Tincture of Digitalis, a heart medicine (3/6 a pound). Pick the seeds from the pod of the purple foxglove, starting after the flower has died down, and pack into a tin with a well-fitting lid.'

Some herbs were sent through the Red Cross to prisoners of war in an attempt to relieve the monotony of their diet. Hutton WI received a talk from Mrs Harrison on herbs and how to use them in wartime. Mrs Harrison became responsible for making the herb garden at Denman College; she was already famous for having preferred a copy of *Culpepper's Herbal* to a diamond ring as a silver wedding present from her husband.

Something out of nothing

Members of Hutton WI, like many other villagers, brought their own spoonful of tea to monthly meetings during the war. Much time was taken up by 'make-do-and-mends' and talks on how to 'make something useful out of nothing'. They heard from Miss Guest, who spoke on the Canadian WI: 'We could not but be proud of our colonies when we heard how splendidly the women of an institute in Canada had sent to the Motherland huge quantities of canned fruit and chickens for the use of the troops.' Many WIs received gifts from sister institutes in Canada, Australia and other countries away from the theatre of war.

At home, in Hutton, the children collected two pounds and six ounces of wool from the hedgerows and Mrs Morgan collected 800 pounds of gooseberries. Tomato plants were distributed, grown from seed sent from Canada.

Rabbit breeding was encouraged, both for food and fur. Goat keeping, too, became popular and a special WI leaflet was published giving sensible advice on how to choose and maintain a goat. It was suggested that a 'sufficient love of' the animal was vital to good goat-keeping. There was a reward for the successful, as one member discovered: 'I didn't know what a good cup of tea was till I kept my goats,' she said.

Even more popular was pig-keeping. Pig clubs were formed: one thousand within the first year, 1941. With a regal flourish, the one-thousandth club was formed by members of the Royal Household at Windsor Castle.

Another leaflet gave excellent advice on food planning in wartime. There were suggestions for stinging nettle purée, on how to clarify fat, on haybox cookery and tripe custard. If things get really bad, why not resort to 'hard-time omelet', which 'makes bacon and eggs go a long way round'?

Village WIs concentrated on campaigns to collect scrap iron. Waste paper was also gathered, to be pulped and remade into tubes for the inside of shells, mines and bombs, boxes for cartridges and gas masks, boarding for the inside of army huts, drums for cables. Bones were collected from which to extract glycerine for use in explosives, glue and fertilizers. (Six old bills made one washer for a shell, one envelope made fifty cartridge wads, one nine-inch enamelled saucepan made a bayonet, two three-pint tin kettles made a steel helmet, one broken garden fork plus a ten-and-a-half-inch enamelled pail made a tommy gun, two four-inch flat irons made six hand grenades, and six-and-a-half pounds of rubber made an airman's dinghy and could save his life.)

Handicrafts were taught to billeted troops and to soldiers in hospital; a letter-friend scheme was started with American country women; WI ambulances were formed. Members got in the harvest, hoed turnips, 'mothered lovely land girls', opened first aid stations, gave blood, started troop canteens and made garments for refugees in Europe. In Somerset,

Herbs were a source of much-needed drugs during the last war. Here members of a WI Culinary Herb Drying Centre pose with some home produced herbs.

one village WI adopted the crews of three ships and made 13,000 garments for them. Another WI worked a laundry for 950 soldiers. A third raised £20,509 for National Savings.

A certain Mrs Stephens discovered the adaptability of her pram. It was used on flag days to transport her four young children, thereby shamelessly winning both sympathy and money. She pushed the children up to the common but on the way back the pram was full of blackberries for jam. She wheeled it round the farms and returned with it full of scrap metal. She turned it into a delivery pram for the 'meat pie' scheme for farm workers. She may even have used it when she attended the WI market in Henley-on-Thames.

Mrs Beale, on the other hand, recalls the member who slipped upstairs from the shelter during an air-raid and did the washing up from the tea that had been so rudely interrupted. But Mrs Evans had a sadder tale to tell. It was 1945 when she wrote her Tea Report:

> *'The struggle now is over,*
> *We have crushed the Jap and Hun,*
> *Does this mean pre-war cake again?*
> *No fear! We still have bun.'*

There was much planning to be done before the struggle ended. There were new ideas on social justice in the air. Sir William Beveridge published his 'Report on Social Insurance and Allied Services' in 1942. In a way, this was Britain's declaration of war aims – the look to a better future – and it became the basis, or ideal, for the welfare state. The WI studied the report. They filled out a questionnaire for the Scott Committee, on which Lady Denman herself sat. The Committee sought to find out if inadequate housing in the villages was a cause of the drift to the towns.

They also filled out a questionnaire for the Dudley Committee, on the features considered essential for every house. They listened to the Uthwatt Report, which proposed the nationalization of land values and control of the siting of factories. They expressed great interest in the Town and Country Planning Act of 1944, which endured much subsequent amendment. And they listened with even keener interest to Mr Butler's Education Act, the same year.

'What has post-war planning to do with winning the war?' asked *Home and Country*. There was no need to look further than the next paragraph for the answer. Victory was a question of faith, said the article, therefore planning was essential. Life would be very different after the war and village WIs should know what they wanted.

Turning to China as an example, *Home and Country* commended 'the most wonderful reconstruction going on right in the midst of war . . . Japan is fighting not an army but an entire population. If our whole nation has that unity it will also be unconquerable. Although fighting desperately against an enemy vastly superior in equipment and training the Chinese are rapidly developing the interior of their country. Students of blitzed universities have tramped hundreds of miles carrying their books and are now passing on knowledge to the uneducated masses. Health services, co-operative stores, are making life infinitely more worthwhile for thousands of humble villagers.' Adelaide Hoodless might well have raised her hand in greeting over the miles and the years.

There was no better time to put WI intentions into practice than wartime. Their intentions were to make life more worthwhile – for themselves and for others. Speaking at their 1943 AGM, the queen said, 'When we have won through to peace, a great page in the history of Britain's war effort should be devoted to the country women in this dear land of ours.' Adopting a more official pose, a government white paper concluded that 'the high degree of mobilization in this war has been largely due to the contribution made by women'.

Hutton WI provided a postscript to the war. 'God Save the King' was sung before each monthly wartime meeting. When war was over, God and the king returned to their peacetime place, at the end of proceedings. They had done their bit. Common sense had won the day.

Food for the nation

'DIGGING for victory' was a spadework spirit that survived the war. Mr Attlee's post-war Labour government, intent on nationalization, class unity and the respectability of Labour, came to power on the promise of co-ordinated action for the future. But what of the present? Taxation remained at a wartime high and the watchword was 'austerity'.

Bread and potatoes were rationed for the first time. A fuel shortage made even more uncomfortable the severe winter of 1946/47. The Dior 'New Look', with swirling skirts and small waists, challenged the girls to keep up with fashion despite continued clothing coupons. As chancellor of the exchequer, Sir Stafford Cripps battled with inflation, which he and his colleagues fought to control with full employment and an export drive. For once, in peacetime, the general public were solidly behind their efforts. As always, the WI were willing and eager to work.

Operation Produce was launched in 1947. The target was ten pounds of extra food from each WI member. Topping the list of successes was the 86-year-old who grew 36 marrows from two plants. Estimates of surplus were not easy to make for it was difficult to divide the average from the extra amount of produce. Judging by their traditional modesty, it may be assumed that the official figures published by the WI are only a fraction of the total effort. There was cause for pride in 100 extra pig clubs, 313 rabbit clubs (with 5161 rabbit keepers), 204 extra goat keepers, 384 new colonies of bees, an extra 2000 tons of potatoes and vegetables and a total of 31,000 new fruit trees.

Greedy
for instruction

Interest in growing, cooking and preserving had been built into the birth of the WI. They were fundamental parts of the country woman's way of life. Preservation began in the First World War, during the autumn of 1916, when Mr Yerburgh of the AOS imported six sterilizing outfits from the United States. The newly-founded WIs quickly came to grips with these technological marvels and became greedy for further instruction. In the first annual report of the National Federation, it was noted that nearly every one of the 199 WIs had enjoyed a bottling demonstration and several had established village bottling centres.

As a further example of interest in produce, it was also reported in 1917/18 that 'cheese was made at Mr Egremont's Farm and sold at Mrs Urqhart's every Saturday by members of the WI. Queues were so great that they demanded police control.'

Despite the lean time when government interest in agriculture lagged during the 1920s, the natural enthusiasm of the WI kept local interest sufficiently alive to benefit from the increased practical instruction in the 1930s. This was sparked off by the Denman Report of 1928, by the committee of which Lady Denman was the chairman. The Report was primarily concerned with the 'practical education of women for rural life' and emphasized the dual nature of the woman's role in growing the produce outdoors and cooking it indoors. Knowledge of one skill, said Lady Denman, was little use without the other. Quite properly, the Report was made a subject for special study by the WI.

It had already been shown that village WIs needed an occasional reprimand. Miss Simpson reported that there were more than 250 exhibits in produce at the Royal Show of 1927. Standards showed an improvement on the previous year, 'especially in bacon and eggs, potted fruit, vegetables, game and poultry, all of which were exceptionally good and attracted

considerable attention.' However, Miss Simpson was displeased with the jams, which 'were not all as good as they ought to have been', and plainly irritated by the jam-makers themselves, who 'should label their jams properly and not write on the cover; the prick of a pen on the cover may puncture it and cause air leakage'.

Eat good food

Standards rose when official encouragement came to their aid; by 1930 the WI had their first instructress in rural domestic economy. It was a time of national depression once again and the WI were told the best way they could help, as in every crisis, was 'to produce good food, to eat good food, to conserve good food

The WI markets – of which this stall is a splendid early example – were started to help the unemployed and disabled ex-servicemen but the idea of stalls for country women dates back to the time of Charles I.

and to market good food'. They had work to do.

'Buy British' ordered their chairman, or keep a few extra hens. Twenty million eggs were still being imported into Britain, even though, in 1930, there were 47 million poultry in the country. That was double the number of poultry known to be scratching away at the land in 1921 and about 20 million more than the higher pre-war figure of 1913.

The WI were only too well aware of the dangers of relying on imports. The First World War had been a lesson they were unlikely to forget. They remembered discussing the subject of rabbits – 'an utterly neglected source of

Food for the nation

income in this country'. Germany was then the largest rabbit meat producer while England, in 1914, was importing 11,000 tons of tame rabbit meat for food. Hardly a year passed in which at least one issue of *Home and Country* did not contain an article on rabbit-breeding.

County produce exhibitions raised their tent poles during the 1930s and, between 1934 and 1938, there were several two-day schools in judging produce, held by the National Federation. In 1937, a big rural domestic economy 'Growing for Cooking' conference was attended by County Federation representatives.

WI market pavilion at the 1976 Royal Agricultural Show.

Two years later, on the verge of war, a Produce Guild was formed, first mooted as early as 1927. The Ministry of Agriculture contributed £500 for development. This Guild, which lasted until 1972, was responsible during the war for providing members with 140,000 fruit bushes and 134,000 approved packets of vegetable seeds. It also helped to teach WI members how to get better results from their gardens through more intensive cultivation, crop rotation and a wider use of vegetables in the family menu.

Villages did not always sound grateful for the Guilds. Visiting one WI, Helena Deneke was presented to the members. 'No one in this village wants to hear about Produce Guilds,' said the president. 'Miss Deneke has come to speak about them tonight.'

While keeping in practice at the annual Royal Show, members have enjoyed two big post-war exhibitions of produce: the produce Exhibition of 1948 and the Country Feasts and Festivals Competition of 1962. Early rounds of Country Feasts at local and county level took nearly two years, culminating in a final judg-

ing at the Olympia Dairy Show. Exhibitions of country fare illustrated historical feasts and traditional festivals such as the Seasons, Christmas, Hallowe'en, Harvest Home and Easter, as well as local festivals.

The winning WI was Ashcott and Pedwell, in Somerset, who presented a 'Feast for the Waits' – a 'gem of Victoriana, staging an informal buffet supper of mid-Victorian period set in a large Somerset Country house, with hot and cold food to welcome weary Waits after singing and playing in the streets' – all this in a space not exceeding six feet by three feet.

Going to market

Cramped quarters are quite common for the WI at work. Their markets may be forced to squeeze into the corner of a hall, find space where they can in a crowded village square or gain protection from the side of a van. On the other hand, they may take over an entire shop.

The markets are the shop-front of the WI, the point at which members and non-members mingle to buy and sell their produce and spend a pleasant hour or two in friendly chatter. This corner-shop atmosphere is encouraged by the market-stall, where market-goers know they can buy fresh produce, well-prepared, delicious home-made cakes and jams, bottled fruits and flowers picked that morning, brought in early from the surrounding countryside – all clearly and pleasantly presented and sold with a smile.

There is only one disadvantage to the buyer. The reputation of the markets means that most of the produce goes in the first hour. Buyers must rise as early to get what they want as sellers must to get it ready. The sellers themselves aren't complaining. According to Claire Balmer, who is National Marketing Organizer, they consider themselves the luckiest people in the WI. *The Times* decided in 1966 that the WI market stall was 'one of the most successful and valuable of our British institutions'.

Market figures support that claim. At the beginning of 1976, there were 310 markets, spread throughout every county in England and Wales. These produced an annual turnover of more than £1¼ million, of which over £1 million went back into the pockets of the men and women who had grown, baked and bottled their way to some very useful extra cash. That is a large shop-window. It is not surprising that many people first hear of the WI through the market-stall.

What many people do not know is that you don't have to be a member of the WI to sell your extra produce at the market. This unique country co-operative is open to the unemployed or the old-age pensioner, to the house-bound cook or the active gardener, to the woman who would like to bake an extra cake once every two weeks or the Newport WI market controller who baked 300 cakes a week. It is also open to men.

What you do with your profit is your own concern. The few extra pence brought in from surplus blackberries, from a glut of curly kale or some fresh, home-baked scones were often, in the beginning, the first money a woman could call her own – an important step in self-esteem and a feeling of independence if all her money had hitherto come from her husband. Making the most of her small patch of garden enabled one widow to keep her children at home instead of sending them into care. One mother saved enough to visit her daughter *twice* in Australia; another travelled to Canada on her homespun profits.

A few pounds a month can augment an inadequate pension, help restock and fertilize a garden, buy boots for children, enable an isolated villager to run a car, buy gadgets for the home. A blacksmith and a potter were both able to set themselves up in business by supplementing their income through the WI markets. In some cases the money fills a real need; in other cases it provides pleasant luxuries. There was one bride who was able to buy real lace to put on her undies with the money she made from surplus soft fruit in the farm garden. Another hard-smoking marketeer paid for all her cigarettes with garden produce.

Self-help

The markets were started to help the unemployed and disabled ex-servicemen but WI market-stalls go back, in theory, to the time of Charles I, when a charter was given to the country women around Berwick-on-Tweed allowing them to bring their produce to sell in the town. There is a 20th-century WI market in

Berwick today. Many other modern markets carry on long traditions stretching back hundreds of years.

A market of a slightly different kind opened to wholesalers at Criccieth, in Caernarvonshire, as a 'fourth line of defence' against the food shortage of 1916/17. But this ran into opposition from local retailers who claimed it was undercutting them and the market closed in 1927. The first real WI market started at Lewes, in East Sussex, in 1919, to provide a much-needed outlet for the produce of the nearby Ringmer Land Settlement for ex-servicemen. We can assume that the market fulfilled its purpose because the first year's turnover was £1176 18s 2d. Produce was sold at ordinary retail prices – a practice that is followed today.

Fourteen years later, the Bath market tried a similar experiment when it arranged to sell the produce of the Timsbury Smallgrowers Association. Timsbury was a mining village which suffered high unemployment during the Depression. The market opened small but positive opportunities for cottage gardeners, allotment holders, the unemployed and the old-age pensioners, who lived on next-to-nothing.

There was some suspicion of the early markets among the WI. Many called the marketeers 'shameless' and said they should be feeding their children, not scrabbling for profit. Others feared that standards might lapse without proper control and bring the good name of the WI into disrepute, for the markets were independent of the National Federation, which had little idea of their extent.

In spite of opposition, villagers welcomed the markets. By 1921, seven counties had one or more stalls, some large, some very small. Many collapsed for lack of backing from the National Federation but numbers steadily grew and by 1932 some of the more flourishing could boast annual turnovers of £2000 or £3000.

It was in 1932 that the Ministry of Agriculture approached the WI to expand the markets and form a National Marketing Organization with a view to helping the unemployed from the Depression. Appropriately, it was the East Sussex Federation – home of the Lewes market

In 1936 German troops occupied the Rhineland (see our picture) and the King of England abdicated to marry an American divorcee. The world was not what it used to be. But the WI were determined to retain their sanity and plan for a better future, even in the turmoil of war. It was just as important to win the peace, they reasoned, and there were many who agreed.

In 1936 Hitler occupied the demilitarized zone of the Rhineland. The French and British made no protest — yet Stanley Baldwin himself had called the Rhine 'Britain's modern frontier'.

In America Roosevelt's New Deal was in full swing. In Britain Victor Gollancz started his Left Book Club. The Italians captured Addis Ababa, the capital of Ethiopia, and the brave little Emperor Hailie Selassie went into exile. In Spain General Franco emerged and the major powers agreed not to intervene in Spain's Civil War. Of course, true to form, the totalitarian powers did exactly the reverse. The Soviets aided the Republicans and Germany and Italy backed the fascist Franco.

This was the year of King Edward VIII's abdication, the year of Mrs Simpson. The British, totally absorbed by a really sensational scandal, sought relief by preparing for the coronation of the new king, George VI

FOOTPATHS

Whitecross WI, Cornwall, had few doubts where the true interests of all right-thinking Britishers lay — clearly in the preservation of footpaths around the coast formally patrolled by coastguards. These footpaths, declared their resolution, should be preserved for public use and enjoyment.

Before much could be done about the resolution, the Second World War had to be fought but the WI returned ruthlessly to the theme in 1948 when Cambo WI, in Northumberland, urged the government of the day to carry through the public footpath recommendations contained in an 'Access to the Countryside'

Committee's report, adding — with typical British caution in these matters — 'provided that the interests of the owners of the land are safeguarded'. After all, there must be balance in all things.

The WI's footpath pressure group's activities were successful. In 1948 the National Parks and Access to the Countryside Act became law and a national survey of footpaths was begun in 1950. Most county councils have now produced their definitive maps.

NURSES

1938 — the year of Munich and the Czech crisis, of Neville Chamberlain's 'Peace in our time' — a year in which the WI turned part of its attention to the bad conditions endured by nurses. Only twelve months away from the greatest war in history, when nurses were to be more vital than ever, they were still poorly paid, badly housed and worked long, exhausting hours. Caernarvonshire Federation welcomed a government inquiry into the profession and stressed the need for shorter hours, better pay and better conditions generally.

CARE OF CHILDREN

A resolution moved by Northamptonshire Federation's Executive Committee only four months before Britain went to war with Germany makes ironic reading in retrospect. The WI was quite properly concerned about the dangers of leaving children 'of tender years alone in a house'. They believed every effort should be made to rouse public opinion.

Only a few months after this resolution was carried in May, 1939,

far worse things were to happen to the world's children. And to the world's parents, too.

Nevertheless, the WI's campaign had its effect. Under the Children and Young Persons' Act of 1952, a fine can be imposed if a child under twelve is killed or suffers serious injury by being allowed to be in a room with an insufficiently guarded open fire or heating appliance.

EQUALITY OF EDUCATION

During the early years of the war the WI, like every other individual and organization in Britain, was too involved with the problems of the violent present to give much thought to the problems of peace. But in 1943 it was possible to organize an AGM and mandates were once more authorized by the members. By 1943 victory was in sight. People's thoughts began to turn towards the sort of world they would like to see after the war.

There had, of course, been a revolution in thinking. Many of the social barriers had come tumbling down. The soldiers, sailors and airmen were determined that the next peace should be better than the last and their womenfolk were equally resolute.

A motion on education put forward by Newdigate WI, Surrey, fully reflects the new mood — equality of opportunity.

Clearly, Britain was not prepared to return to the blatant inequalities of the pre-war world.

The NFWI's campaign for a full nursery school system is now appreciated as an essential aspect of a sound educational system. Yet even by 1972 less than 35 per cent of four-year-olds received education in maintained schools for even part of their fifth year — and for three-year-olds the proportion was a mere five per cent. Now the plan is for nursery school facilities to be provided for up to 90 per cent of four-year-olds and 50 per cent of three-year-olds by 1982, mainly on a part-time basis and without charge.

EQUAL PAY

But education was only one of 1943's resolutions. There were — not surprisingly, after the enormous efforts of women during the war — the first rumblings of 'women's lib'. Bures WI, West Suffolk, put forward a resolution 'that men and women should receive equal pay for equal work' and again the movement's commandos went into action. This resolution went off to the Ministry of Labour, Education and the Treasury, the FBI and the TUC.

The campaign was maintained. In 1944 evidence was submitted to the Royal Commission on Equal Pay and for many years afterwards the WI — today regarded by extremists on the 'liberation' front as mildly establishment and middle-class — was represented on the Equal Pay for Equal Work Campaign Committee.

BEVERIDGE REPORT

The WI was firmly behind the Beveridge report which laid the foundations of the welfare state. A resolution recorded the movement's appreciation of his great work for social security and particularly his recognition of the fact that health insurance for housewives and children's allowances were essential if family life was to be free from want. This appreciative resolution came from Toft WI, Cheshire.

POST WAR AID

The WI took a positive view of the contribution it believed women could make in building up the post-war world. Essex Federation moved that the NFWI should consider ways and means by which the WIs could help in the immediate post-war relief of Europe. In 1944 the NFWI Committee accepted an invitation from the Ministry of Supply to help in a scheme for making garments for distribution by the military authorities and by UNRRA in liberated Europe. More than 250,000 garments were knitted by WI members before the scheme came to an end in 1945. In 1960 a total of £75,000 collected by the WIs was handed over to the UK Committee for the World Refugee Year. Again the WI demonstrated that it did not just pass resolutions but actually *did* things.

– that proposed the resolution at the Albert Hall that set up this Organization. One thousand pounds was contributed by the Carnegie United Kingdom Trust to help establish the markets over the first four years and to pay for a national organizer, on condition that the markets remained open to non-members as well as members, men as well as women.

In September, Miss Vera Cox was appointed as organizer. There were about thirty markets when she began. By the war, there were about 100 markets. There were 160 markets with an annual turnover of £$\frac{1}{4}$ a million by the time she retired in 1963.

The markets remain independent of the National Federation since the construction of the NFWI does not permit trading activities which bring personal gain to members. The members themselves are registered under the Industrial and Provident Societies Act as friendly societies. All producers become shareholders in their society or belong to an organization holding a trustee share. In 1932, anyone could take up a share for one shilling. Today, one share remains at only five pence for life.

Annual contributions are made to National Federation funds, in return for which the markets receive advice and instruction from headquarters. They now make a contribution of one per cent on the first £2000 of turnover and half a per cent on anything over that. This brings in about £8000 a year to the National Federation. The producers themselves pay about ten per cent of their sales receipts toward the expenses both of the local market and the county marketing organization.

Tin hats among the cabbages

Miss Cox still comes up to London for the annual marketing conference, even though she is about eighty. She admits that she learnt the job as she went along and was terrified at the prospect of organizing the markets. It was hard work at first but they came into their own with the war. In 1939 no new shops were allowed to open and everyone was encouraged to cover up their tennis courts and grow more food, 'though no one had any idea how to get rid of the extra produce'. This illogicality was officially recognized and new markets were reluctantly allowed to open. These helped to meet the sudden influx of refugees which swelled the size of the villages to alarming proportions.

Rabbits and pigeons became increasingly popular on the market stall and prams were often used for transport. High standards were maintained and, far from remembering the problems or fears of those times, Miss Cox recalls the home-guard spirit and the ridiculous accidents – the air-raid wardens doubling as market controllers and losing their tin hats among the cabbages. As in so many aspects of life, the WI were able to rise above the insanity of the age and restore life's equilibrium.

The markets reached a peak of 300 by the end of the war, after which post-battle exhaustion caused a decline. To revive their flagging wares, they received an invitation to hold a market at the Ideal Home Exhibition in the Coronation Year of 1953. The stall they had proved an Everest of achievement – with all the effort and all the success met with by the expedition that scaled that mountain the same year. The marketeers excelled themselves.

For a whole month, those nearest London supplied the stall with fresh farm produce which had to be in Central London by eight in the morning or late at night to avoid the rush. 'Fathers came up in the morning with cream in their brief-cases; brothers made special journeys from East Kent to rugger matches and stopped off with ginger bread and cauliflowers; one Guernsey pilot came over especially from the Channel Islands, the only time, he said, that his wife was happy to see him go.'

A sudden frost killed the first replacements of daffodils from Hampshire but a phone call brought further replacements from Devon within 24 hours. One market controller was suddenly taken to hospital for an operation. After seeing her in, her husband cycled ten miles at half past ten at night to give the necessary produce to the steward who was taking it up to London, so that when his wife came out of the anaesthetic he could tell her not to worry.

The exhibition was a triumph for the markets. The *Manchester Guardian* thought they were the best thing in Olympia. 'Londoners found it difficult to realize,' wrote Miss Cox, 'that preserves and cakes had really been made by what they called "ordinary people".' There were fruit and vegetables that had been stored through the winter (the exhibition was in March), salads brought on under cloches, spring flowers, bowls of bulbs, alpines, cacti, honey, beeswax and honey vinegars, jams, jellies, marmalades, bottled and canned fruit, home-made brawns, sausages, sauces, pickles, ketchups, relishes, poultry, all kinds of eggs including those of geese, hens, ducks and blue-green eggs from a South American hen, cheeses, bread, cakes, toys, baskets and pasties.

Value
for money

In 1958 and 1961, there were two more large markets at the Ideal Home Exhibition and in 1965 an even larger one to celebrate the Golden Jubilee. Nearly £4000 went back to the marketeers at the 1958 exhibition, in payment for anemones from Cornwall, turkeys from Bath, marmalade from Jersey, heather honey from Northumberland, and a great range of goods from 33 contributing counties. From the cheerful-sounding jam called 'High Dumpsie Dearie' to a carefully made basket small enough to hold one Easter egg, what impressed visitors most was the quality, peculiar to the WI, of the truly home-made set off with a professional touch.

'Nothing but the best at the WI market,' said one paper at the 1965 exhibition. 'A friendly chat and value for money,' said another. Market reputations spread abroad. One sent snowdrops to Denmark and Paris, Lent lilies to Sweden.

In 1976, at the annual Royal Show, produce came in from such varying directions as Cumberland, Taunton, Winchester and Surrey. In the last two years the markets have increased at a rate of about 24 a year. The smallest has a turnover of about £15; an average is between £30 and £150 a week. In two and a half hours selling each week, the Andover market turns over £17,000 a year. Some markets remain open five days a week.

Transport is a problem once more, as it was in the beginning. Some members believe the solution lies in opening more, smaller markets among the villages. Another problem has been to get members to observe the necessary bureaucracy of proper labelling, insisted on by the National Federation to comply with statutory regulations. 'It doesn't look home-made,' complain the culprits. There have been criticisms as well as praise from the press but rules and standards are strictly enforced and slipshod presentation is not accepted by the market controller.

There has, too, been the occasional criticism by other traders that markets provide unfair competition. But the WI do not try to undercut existing traders and, on the whole, they offer a very different product. In some cases, complaints have started only when a market has disappeared: when the market closed in Forest Row, local traders asked for it to return because their own purchasers had been drawn off to a larger town. It is agreed that markets provide a useful incentive to general trade, attracting customers who spend their money at other stores as well.

'I don't know what I'd do without a market,' said one seller to Miss Balmer, who sees them as an important fount of mutual benefit and understanding. Mrs Jacob agrees that 'markets and institutes are pieces of the National Federation jig-saw which must be fitted together if the whole is to benefit'. Miss Gray sees the public relations value of the markets – an open forum of views between the public and the WI.

A marketeer once phoned up her market organizer in a panic on the morning of the market to say that she had mislaid the hard-boiled egg she had prepared for breakfast. Could someone check through the *eight dozen* fresh eggs she'd sent for sale? Market organizers have to expect that sort of crisis. They take orders for wedding garments and cakes for special occasions. They helped acclimatize their customers to the agonies of decimalization and they are now smoothing out the intricacies of metrication for customers and marketeers.

Some of their best customers do not come from the WI at all. Some of the very best are widowers in search of the lost delights of home cooking and the busy friendliness of the market stall, where those behind the counter are known to be as good value as their product.

Old skills, new excellence

'ARTY-CRAFTY' worthiness and the symbol of the 'raffia hat' – these contributed to the unfortunate image fostered by contemptuous public opinion, which early members scorned in their enthusiasm. Handicrafts, like markets and produce, became shop-windows to the institutes, and the public, seeing their exhibitions, soon learnt to respect the excellence of their work.

When the Industrial Revolution lured so many people to the towns and turned their hands to the manufacture of machines, the village became the last outpost of the old crafts that could only be made to traditional standards by hand and with the aid of time and skill. In many country districts, skills disappeared completely. The WI provided the necessary meeting place where they could be discussed and revived.

Inez Jenkins remembers there were few teachers at first. Knowledge was mutually exchanged. Crafts were passed on from friend to friend. If your grandmother had taught you how to make leather gloves, you were happy to teach someone else.

Handicrafts quickly became a popular aspect of WI activity. As early as the summer of 1917, a small exhibit of work was shown at a National Economy Exhibition in Hyde Park. Queen Mary was greatly interested and toy making was encouraged by the popularity of Cuthbert, a rabbit copied from the well-known contemporary cartoon.

Very soon, there was talk among the National Executive that the skills acquired in toy-making, rug and basket-making, dyeing, weaving and gloving should be turned toward establishing local industries that would contribute to the revival of local communities. A sub-committee was set up to look into the commercial possibilities but advised against the idea. Instead, the Guild of Learners was begun in 1920 to encourage the development of home crafts. Its aims were twofold: 'to regain the practice of home handicrafts with a view to restore the best traditions of English workmanship' and 'to assist in bringing the best instruction in handicrafts within the reach of the villages'.

The Guild was immediately popular. Whereas the report on local industries had stated that 'the great bulk of institute members has neither the time nor the inclination to feed a market', the villagers were very interested in practising and perfecting their skills. A system of tests was adopted – 'A' for proficiency, 'B' for lecturers and demonstrators, 'C' for teachers and judges – and the first school was held at Tunbridge Wells, with instruction in carpentry, upholstery, curing of skins, the making of baskets and gloves, spinning and weaving. To help the schools, the Development Commission gave annual grants.

In the matter of rabbit *skins* – a subject of discussion as popular as rabbit *meat* – it was pointed out that France imported British rabbits and returned them to Britain ready dressed and made into clothes. This waste of British resources was condemned. Could not Britain's women cure and craft British fur!

Dyeing was another early craft. Mrs Nugent Harris had a story of the WI member who left a demonstration to beg a jug of boiling water from a neighbour. 'There's a lady dyeing in our Institute,' she said, to which the neighbour sensibly replied 'Surely a drop of brandy 'ud be better.'

By the 1930s, schools concentrated on teaching the teachers, who passed on their knowledge to the village WIs. There were schools in methods of teaching, judging and demonstrating, all aimed at upholding the standards of work produced by the Guild and in consequence setting a standard for country skills

for everyone to see. In an unpublished essay on the WI, Doris Cumming wrote that early members 'were in fact creating the first constructive attitude to quality in all their activities and exercising their powers of discrimination, which has proved to be one of their greatest assets'.

Something very special

First among their assets were the women who guided them. Handicrafts had their own share of founding characters. Mrs Nugent Harris always took an active interest. Lady Denman was rather less interested. She would bring large groups of friends to the exhibitions and, according to the ever-observant Mrs Otter,

Crafts and all sorts of skills were grist to the WI mill. Here we see a tinkering class in session and women learning shoe mending at Scynes Hill (Sussex) Institute.

'was obviously immensely proud of the superb work, although the rumour was that she rather despised handicrafts; she rarely appeared at crafts sub-committees, said little and smoked throughout'.

Clearly, handicrafts needed strong support, which they got from Miss Armes, who set high standards and possessed a certain ruthlessness and the courage necessary to maintain those standards. During her time at headquarters she built up the tradition that WI handicrafts were something very special. Her faith rested in the belief that the skill of the old crafts was still in the hands of the country women.

Old skills, new excellence

Neither she nor the country women always found each other easy to get on with. Her north country obstinacy and their pride often clashed, to the delight of Mrs Otter, who remembers how unpopular Miss Armes had made herself when judging a Nottingham exhibition of handicrafts. Apparently, there was a crinoline lady's nightdress case, made in paper, which, though much admired, Miss Armes rejected. To general indignation, she refused to allow it to be shown. The County made it clear they did not wish to see her again. Fortunately, it proved necessary for her to revisit Nottingham some time later. 'I had to use much guile to get her there,' said Mrs Otter. Once there, 'she exerted all her charm' and the County was won over despite itself. Mrs Otter was informed that the County considered that Miss Armes 'had mellowed over the years'.

Mrs Otter had an innocent taste for such conflicts. She remembers, also with relish, clashes that occurred between Miss Armes and Mrs Heron Maxwell, another handicraft stalwart. It was hardly surprising that characters should jar among so many personalities.

Serenely spinning

The public saw none of this. What they did see were the exhibitions, superbly staged by Miss Armes or some other energetic organizer. If they were lucky, they might also catch a glimpse of Miss Somerville sitting in the midst of her stand set prominently by the entrance, 'serenely spinning, hung round with swags of wool in gorgeous colours'.

For those who attended the first two National Exhibitions of 1918 and 1920, there were exhibits to buy. The second made £1000 for members as well as a substantial contribution to the National Federation. Subsequently it was felt that handicrafts were not up to their best standard when prompted by commercial considerations. The first National Handicrafts Exhibition which attempted to show examples only of the highest standard of work was held at the Victoria and Albert Museum in 1922. There were 652 exhibits from 49 counties.

'Only in one or two instances,' bewailed one reporter, 'was excellent work wasted on un-suitable objects. An orang-outang, for instance, beautifully made and perfect in every detail, and positively life-like in its repulsive hideousness, grinned evilly at us for three days on end. A child would need strong nerves to take such a toy to bed . . .'

Mothers needed strong nerves also. Staging such exhibitions involved innumerable headaches and a high degree of organizational ability. These were not 'arty-crafty' parish shows. Up to the war, there were exhibitions at Drapers Hall, the City of London, the Indian Pavilion, the Imperial Institute and the New Horticultural Hall, Westminster, where, for the first time, in 1932, there were exhibits from every County Federation. All these drew large crowds of visitors.

Although the exhibits were of a generally high standard, many represented no more than the normal, careful work of country women, the sort of work they had been doing for years, as one reporter overheard: 'An order from an artist for quilts which he said were "most beautiful" drew from a north-country woman standing by the remark, "Queer how much store the folks down here set on our quilts. We think them just ordinary."' But in 1927, the visiting *Montreal Gazette* thought the quality of work 'almost incredible'. And in 1935, one critical observer was heard to make this comparison: 'One thing I am certain of, the steward's overalls were *not* made by an Institute worker!'

Superb craftswomen

Crafts turned to more practical things during the war. Besides teaching handicrafts to soldiers in hospitals, WI knitters made garments for Europe to keep troops and refugees warm. By 1945, 152,044 garments had been knitted, with Norfolk topping the county league at 9940 garments, half as many again as Hampshire, the runner-up.

A post-war treat was provided in 1951, when members designed their perfect house for the

Queen Mary at the 1917 exhibition in Hyde Park; an upholstery class in Brecon; and Queen Elizabeth and Mrs Jacob at the 1975 Tomorrow's Heirlooms Exhibition.

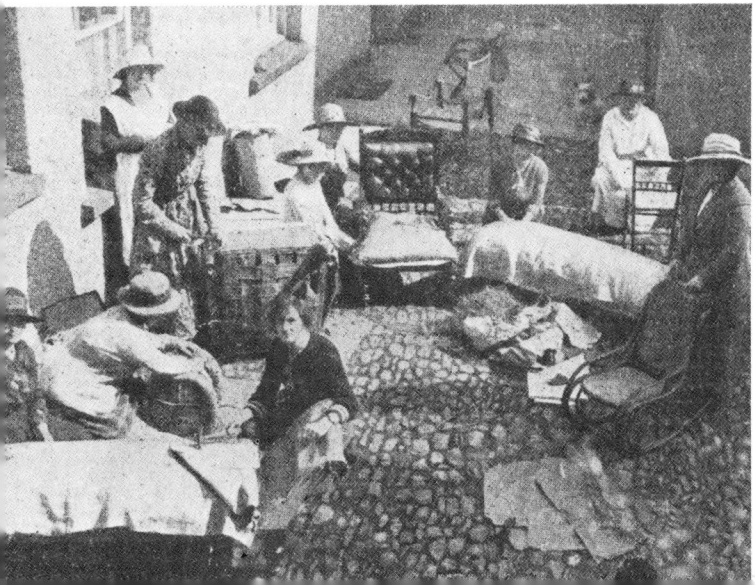

1946–50 : A prod to government

Visitors to children in hospital were restricted between the wars. In 1950 the WI campaigned for more flexible visiting hours. One man who spent years in an open-air hospital similar to this one in the late 1930s says: 'The anguish of monthly visiting was worse than the illness.' The WI set out to change all that and succeeded. The Institutes were also on the warpath about 'the deplorable condition of lavatories' (to say nothing of vandalism) on Britain's railway stations and trains – a problem that is still with us as our picture shows.

VILLAGE HALLS

With its roots in the country's villages the WI has always sought to project village problems and to attract national attention to those problems. In 1945 Pentrevoelas WI, Denbighshire, moved that in post-war planning special attention should be given to the urgent need for well-built, well-lighted and well-equipped public halls in villages and that these should be managed by committees representative of village organizations.

This resolution was sent to the Village Halls Committee of the National Council of Social Service and later in the same year ideas on the interior planning of halls were collected through County Federations and submitted to the same Committee, on which the NFWI is represented. All this was splendid 'market research' since it became possible to build up a general picture of the sort of facilities the villages were seeking.

The WI keeps a watchful eye on the village hall question since the possession of one is of fundamental importance to a thriving community.

POSTAL FACILITIES

The movement is also deeply concerned about adequate postal facilities in villages. Madron WI, Cornwall, reflected the general concern about the closure of rural sub-post offices and a resolution was sent in 1945 to the postmaster general, urging him to improve the status and pay of sub-postmasters and sub-postmistresses.

This was a resolution close to the fundamentals of WI thinking and the campaign was vigorously maintained.

Chignalls and Mashbury WI, Essex, moved a resolution in 1971 urging the minister of posts and telecommunications to examine the problems behind the closure of so many village sub-post offices. The resolution pointed out once again the hardship caused by such closures and urged remedial action.

VILLAGE SCHOOLS

The WI's role both as a prod to government and a practical help to government in establishing the facts of a situation was well demonstrated in 1963 when the Central Advisory Council for Education, under the chairmanship of Lady Plowden, asked the County Federations to collect evidence on village primary schools from the WIs. An NFWI memorandum was sent to the Plowden Committee in 1964.

But it was in 1946 that the NFWI Executive Committee moved a resolution recognizing the value of the school as a centre of village life and urging the local education authorities to provide, wherever possible, well-equipped and adequately staffed junior schools in the villages.

RAILWAY LAVATORIES

Railways, too, have always interested the WI — or, in recent times, the lack of them in rural areas, thanks to Dr (now Lord) Beeching's ruthless axe which removed railway stations from whole rural communities. But in 1946 Brill WI, Buckinghamshire, was calling the attention of the then railway companies (this was before nationalization) to the inadequate number and deplorable condition of the lavatories in most railway stations and trains in England and Wales and urged the provision of better facilities. The resolution also said that on long-distance trains there should be a special compartment, suitably fitted, where mothers with babies could attend to their needs in privacy.

For good measure the resolution also urged that the Public Health Act in relation to sanitary conveniences should be extended to public conveniences 'on the premises of a railway'.

HOUSING FOR ELDERLY

This was a year in which the WI's social conscience was much in evidence. From Potters Bar and Little Heath WI, Middlesex, came a resolution urging the movement to

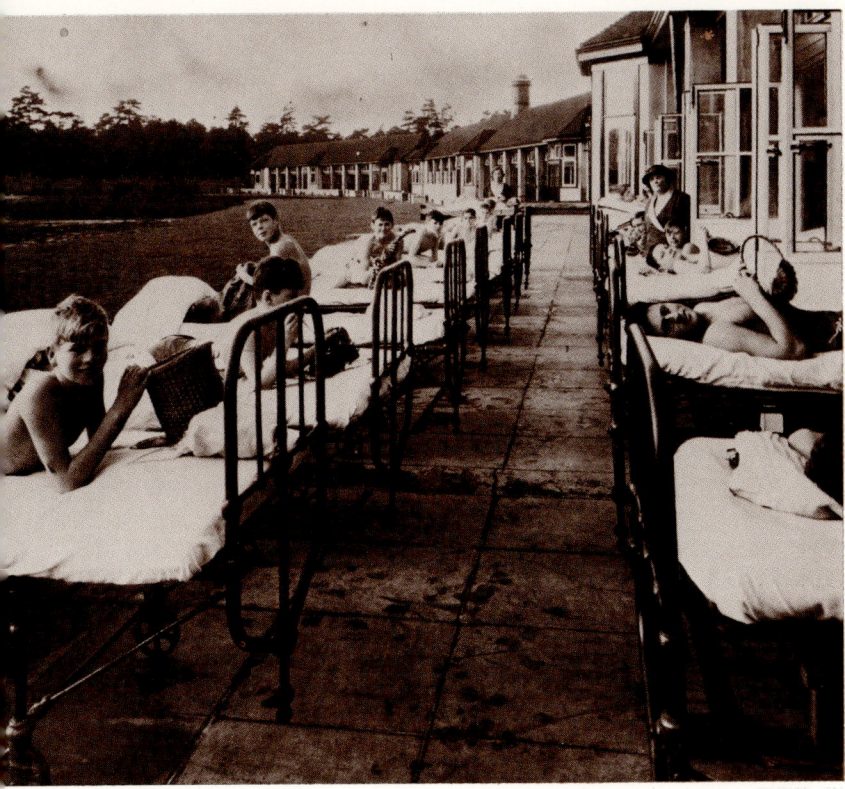

CHILDREN IN HOSPITAL

Anyone who has experienced a long spell in hospital as a child will be eternally grateful to the WI for a resolution passed in 1950. Hampshire Federation, while realizing the difficulties of the nursing staff, deplored the fact that in some hospitals mothers and fathers were not permitted to visit their children. The resolution asked hospital management committees to allow visiting in agreement with doctors and sisters. It was in resolutions of this type that the WI demonstrated the sheer common sense and humanity of ordinary people. Before the rules were changed the orthodox medical view was that children tended to be upset by parental visits. (They did not, of course, consult the children.) In the case of long illnesses the results could be harrowing. Some hospitals even censored letters from the children to their parents in case the homesickness revealed upset the parents!

The Hampshire resolution was sent to the Ministry of Health, to all regional hospital boards and to hospital management committees.

In 1957 the NFWI submitted evidence to the Platt Committee on the Welfare of Children in Hospital which, in its report issued in 1958, recommended that unrestricted visiting by parents should be extended. The NFWI wrote to the minister supporting this and in 1971 a memorandum, based on evidence sent in by the Welsh County Federations and which included comments on visiting hours, was sent to the Welsh Hospital Board.

Today unrestricted visiting, or visiting for the greater part of the day, is permitted by the vast majority of hospitals. An increasing number of hospitals also provide overnight accommodation for the parents of young children. In this one campaign the WI probably did more to promote the happiness of sick children than any other single reform. It was a great victory for common sense and compassion.

draw the attention of the authorities to 'the pressing need' for the housing and care of elderly and lonely people, including the provision of homes of rest for the elderly sick and infirm, financed upon a contributory basis according to means and subsidized by the government.

Many WI members are connected with Age Concern (formerly the National Old People's Welfare Council).

VILLAGE SURGERIES

The WI maintains a constant vigilance over the villages of Britain. Villagers need good medical services just as much as townsfolk and a Nutley WI, East Sussex, resolution of 1947 said that thought should be given in the future planning of villages to the needs of doctors and their surgery patients. It was considered essential that each village should have either a surgery with a waiting room or adequate conveyance to and from the new modern clinics which were to be built in the towns.

The 'new modern clinics' were the health centres provided by local health authorities under the National Health Service Act of 1946. By the end of 1972 about 400 health centres were in operation in England and Wales and some 170 were under construction.

VILLAGE TRANSPORT

Village transport was then — as ever — a problem and Stoke Poges and Wexham WI, Buckinghamshire, demanded in a 1948 resolution that there should be at least a *once a week* bus connection for all villages with their local town. Delegates were urged to ask their WIs to continue to press for this. The resolution also pointed out that buses serving rural areas should not carry short-distance town passengers, or else country people would often be stranded.

In 1964 the County Federations concerned were represented on inquiries into transport in six selected rural areas commissioned by the minister of transport.

Old skills, new excellence

Olympia Ideal Home Exhibition. In the same year, a huge wall-hanging was made, reflecting the activities of country women, to celebrate the Festival of Britain. Members contributed only a small part of the work but the hanging was given to the WI after the exhibition and is now kept in Denman College. It was shown again to the public in 1976, in an exhibition commemorating the 25th anniversary of the Festival.

The greatest post-war craft effort came the next year, 1952, when the Handicraft Exhibition was once again held at the Victoria and Albert Museum, setting out to show the very best of WI work. In that year, there was stiff popular competition from the farewell journey of the last London tram and the opening of

Agatha Christie's *Mousetrap* – still running some 25 years later. The cinemas offered Gary Cooper in *High Noon* and Charlie Chaplin in *Limelight*, but the Exhibition proved to be one of the most popular events in London. Five times the number of expected visitors arrived to admire the work, which included a quilt called 'High Summer' that had taken ten years to make and an embroidered hanging showing the work of women during the war.

In recent years, the largest exhibition of crafts was at the Commonwealth Institute, London, in 1975. The *Sunday Telegraph* remarked of 'Tomorrow's Heirlooms' that 'many professional craftsmen will be surprised at the level of skill in such subjects as sculpture, stone carving and jewellery' and another paper felt that the 'exhibition is a tribute to the skill, patience and imagination of WI members all over the country who have lived up to their reputation of being superb craftswomen'.

There were ceramics, basketry, terracotta figures, wedding dresses, stuffed toys, silverwork, pottery, glass engraving and a variety of hand-made crafts that, as one reporter said, 'probably excels all former efforts to impress (their) real image on the general public'. In April, 1975, a poem appeared in *Home and Country*, especially written by Karl Showler:

'Stand still, and look, and see with all,
What twice ten thousand fingers wrought,
And find in each and every village hall,
Gifts priceless, that no purchase bought.'

There were plenty of practical skills for rural women to develop. These women are making baskets for workmen.

Keeping up to standard

The Guild of Learners had helped to maintain standards and the Loan Collection, which had been available on request, enabled village WIs to see examples of exquisite work without having to travel to museums in London, which many of them could not afford to do. In 1968, a further incentive was introduced in the form of Design Awards. Work in any craft could be submitted to a panel of experts not necessarily drawn from the WI.

The Award is given only to work of the highest standard, of which technical excellence is only considered a part; originality of

The Oxfordshire Federation organized a travelling exhibition of hand industries in 1921 – a progressive and enterprising thing to do in those days.

conception and interpretation are equally important. Writing about the Award in 1971, one craft adviser quoted Lord Clark's 'Civilization', in which he said that, during the Dark Ages, it was arguable that 'Western civilization was saved by its craftsmen'.

The Guild of Learners and the Produce Guild came to an end in 1972. WI members had always been suspicious of 'clubs within clubs' and it was felt that one overall WI membership should embrace all WI activities. Reaction against closing the Guilds was appeased by continuing their activities along much the same lines but in a different context, and under the title of Home Economics.

Home Economics is a phrase that has been universally accepted for some time and covers a wide range of activities. Basic certificates are available in home management and social studies, in cookery, in preservation and wine-making, in gardening, in crafts, in interior design and in planning an exhibition. It is also possible to obtain certain certificates at specialist levels. The purpose of the certificates is to broaden the base of the member's knowledge and to provide an umbrella under which traditional crafts and skills can be carefully

preserved for the future just as they have been saved from the past.

Preparation for the certificates can be tied in with any local education authority, wherever tuition in the required subject is given by the rural home economist of the LEA at formal classes. Members may also make use of correspondence courses or personal experience in Young Farmers' Clubs, local horticultural societies, embroiderers' guilds or whatever may be appropriate. They will also learn a great deal from their own WI lecturers and from courses provided by Denman College.

All this sounds a little daunting but crafts are a lot of fun for WI members. They learn to make curtains or patchwork quilts, they tie-dye and batik, they embroider murals of village scenes or abstracts, they learn to work leather and suede; they work together or work as 'loners' on their own particular interest. But whether or not they exhibit their work or enjoy it at home or show it to their friends, one thing characterizes the pleasure and care they put into that work: 'The WI stands for excellence,' says past General Secretary Miss Withall. 'No matter what it is, it must be as good as it can possibly be made.'

Music, art and drama

NEARLY sixty years ago Miss Nancy Tennant was dragged by her mother to the opening meeting of Ugley WI and thought it a lot of nonsense. There was a talk on hens in which members were told that electric light was essential for the production of eggs. The hens at Miss Tennant's home had been producing very good eggs without benefit of light bulbs for as long as she could remember.

Then she realized that her unsuspecting fellow members could provide her with the raw material for a choir. Music was what she loved best, so she stayed with the WI. Miss Tennant is still a member and in those sixty years much of the musical activity throughout the WI has been due to her enthusiasm. When war broke out and the WI lost Grace Hadow through death and much of Lady Denman's time and attention to the Land Army, Nancy Tennant became vice-chairman of the WI and helped to guide it through the war.

Drawing the net wide

The Welsh origins of the WI ensured an early interest in music and drama. These were also two of the most obviously enjoyable of WI activities and members wasted no time in throwing themselves into performances with customary energy. In 1922, whilst Prokofiev wrote ballet music for Diaghilev, Mr Leslie, a well-known amateur of music from Montgomeryshire, led a class of WI members to the top of a convenient hill, where he taught them descant singing and from which, as one student recalls, 'we had a glorious view that only Wales could unfold'.

Since it was impossible that they had gone there to sing 'Climb Every Mountain' from 'The Sound of Music', which had not yet been written, we must be charitable and can only hope that Mr Leslie had not chosen the site for fear of the disturbance they might otherwise cause to the rest of the village. Reassurance came from another musician, Sir Walford Davies, who 'looked to the Institutes to help to give music its rightful place in our country, not as a professional art but as the natural and universal language of nine hundred and ninety eight people out of every thousand'.

Mr Leslie, not surprisingly, had high expectations. He believed that the WIs should be able 'to develop all the musical talent in the village', particularly in those villagers who 'are fond of music but know nothing about it'. 'Draw the net very wide,' he commanded, 'and do not leave anyone out.'

In that same issue of *Home and Country*, in which Mr Leslie's remarks appeared, there were also articles on WI choirs and 'the dancing English'. There was plenty to learn, as the music teacher found when trying to explain the marks of musical expression to one small boy:

'Now boy,' he said, 'what does *f* mean?'

'Forte, sir.'

'Right, and *ff*?'

'Eighty, sir.'

In 1924, Mr Leslie was especially active on behalf of the WI. He started a one-day school for WI conductors, brought out a special WI Song Book and initiated the singing of 'Jerusalem' at the annual general meeting. There is a story about the choice of song, that Lady Denman used to tell with glee: 'It seemed to some of us,' she said, 'that a competition for an Institute song might produce a good but unknown poetess. Miss Hadow took the view that poetry written for a special purpose was unlikely to be good – but I still hoped. Eventually a verse arrived which started with the line, 'We are a band of earnest women'. This was too much for me, and, as usual, I realized how

The girls have fun in a country festival, and a music course at Denman College on a fine day, taking full advantage of the College's splendid grounds.

right Miss Hadow was – hence "Jerusalem" became and remains the WI song.'

One of the speakers at that 1924 AGM was Grace Hadow's brother, the author of two major reports on adolescent education. Sir Henry Hadow caught the spirit of WI music in a quote from a German musician who had travelled round Europe in the time of Queen Elizabeth I: '"The English" he says "carol; the French sing; the Spaniards weep; the Italians . . . caper with their tongues; but the Germans, which is a shame to say, do howl like wolves." Things have improved a good deal since those early Elizabethan days,' said Sir Henry, 'but I still think that I understand what he meant when he used the word "carolling" for our English singers. There is a sense of personal enjoyment about that word which I believe

that our Elizabethan ancestors had and through which we earned our title of "Merrie England", which of recent years we have been in danger of losing.'

If I can sing . . .

There were those, like the Honourable Mrs Lindley of Somerset, always severe in shirt and tie, who were determined that no such danger should exist for long: 'If I can sing, "We are fairies on the green", I'm sure you can,' she called out boldly to prospective choir members. Others remember early concert parties among the villages with monologues, dances, ballet, minuets, tap hornpipes and singing accompanied by the piano. Choirs from a collection of several villages often went on tour to raise money for charity.

Music was always welcome in the villages – in general more readily welcome than such practical activities as rabbit-curing, as Margaret Deneke found when she doubled as instructress in curing and later, at the same meeting, as musician. 'I did so enjoy your music,' remarked one member afterwards, 'but what a pity we wasted all that time with the woman and the rabbit.'

The pages of *Home and Country* are full of the record of courses for choirs, conductors and instrumental work. Everyone had a lot of fun but nonetheless the work was taken seriously, as one member found who attended a conductor's course, at the end of which, 'no one was allowed to escape without showing the class how much – or how little – she had really profited by what she had seen'.

The war utterly failed to curb musical activity, for music was one good way to make everyone feel a little braver. One correspondent quoted Malcolm Sargent: 'Hitler may make us go short of butter, bacon and sugar – but thank goodness he can't make us go short of our music.' Village WIs emerged from the war singing some recommended lyrics and tunes with ever-improving tone: there was Vaughan Williams' 'Thanksgiving for Victory', 'Greensleeves', Hugh Roberton's 'Hymn to Peace', a variation on Handel 'Pack Clouds Away', and another Vaughan Williams – 'Let Us Now Praise Famous Men'. In November, 1946, singers combined with actors and dancers in the WI Combined Festival of the Arts, which took place in London. If polish was wanting, there was enthusiasm to make up for it.

The music
in their bones

It was Vaughan Williams who was approached to write a special cantata for a WI Singing Festival in 1950, a project which Nancy Tennant had fostered for a long time but which had been cut short by the war and not helped by Lady Denman's relative indifference to WI

music. Miss Tennant's chief supporter had been Grace Hadow.

Preparation for the cantata went on for a year beforehand. Selections were made from 1230 WI choirs, both at county and area level, until 59 choirs combined to make up the single choir of 920 that performed at the Festival with the help of another 2000 singers in the auditorium. 'Folk Songs of the Four Seasons' was performed at the Albert Hall on June 15, with Sir Adrian Boult conducting the London Symphony Orchestra, and was broadcast on 'Woman's Hour'. *The Times* critic acknowledged that it was a 'remarkable achievement', the singers seemed 'to have the music in their bones'.

In 1966, preparations began for another grand singing festival to be held three years later. The subject, according to composer Malcolm Williamson and librettist Ursula Vaughan Williams, 'was to be, broadly, the woman's view of our history – ranging back and forth through the centuries, contrasting the tragedies of widowhood, war, injustice, poverty, with the jubilation of the British woman's achievement, individually and collectively. This then is the Brilliant contrasted with the Dark.'

'The Brilliant and the Dark' was carefully constructed so that it could be sung both in the great area of the Albert Hall, complete with soloists, choir and orchestra, costumes and lighting, or in small sections in village halls to the accompaniment of a piano. Although primarily a musical event, it also contained dramatic impact. For the Albert Hall performance in 1969, about 150 actors and dancers were recruited from WIs in Hertfordshire and East Sussex to perform a magnificent display of dance and mime to illustrate the singing. Their 600 garments were made by members of the WI, from material given by Courtaulds.

As in 1950, there were regional competitions to make the selection for the thousand-strong choir. Accompanied by the English Chamber Orchestra, conducted by Marcus Dods, their performance was much appreciated. 'Effective, often refreshing, sometimes moving', said *The Times*. The *Daily Telegraph* thought the performance 'outstanding'. *The Financial Times* was most struck by the colours of the garments, 'blue and turquoise for the sea sequence, white

The performance of the Brilliant and the Dark at the Albert Hall in 1969 was a chance for the WI to display their sense of theatre and their talent for singing at an almost professional level.

and black for the suffering abbesses, rootless after the Reformation, brilliant greens for the pre-Raphaelite "Summer Dance", airy pastels for "Spring Dance", stark red and white for the Wars of the Roses. Such lavish, flamboyant dresses have not been seen in town for many a day.'

'A mere taster of WI talent for the general public,' was the opinion of *Home and Country*. Determined not to lose the impetus from this event, plans were laid for a WI choir aiming at national recognition and available for concert work of a high standard under the direction of a well-known conductor. This was to be the WI at its most professional, directly in the public eye.

The WI Music Society that resulted from this idea, with the encouragement of conductor Antony Hopkins, had to be careful to achieve the quality it aimed for without weakening the structure of local and more amateur music. It has been criticized for creaming off the best talent; there is a better chance, however, that it has attracted more talent *to* the WI by its reputation. National Chairman Miss Gray welcomed the Society: 'Many of us will be able to say that we were in at the birth of a completely new part of WI life', she said, 'and to be in at the birth of anything is always an exciting occasion.'

As for local enthusiasm, that did not seem to suffer. Oxfordshire had the last word: 'We have

Institutes who said they couldn't sing, then discovered that they could even do part songs. One became so fired with enthusiasm that they went round in tractors broadcasting carols. Unfortunately they ended up in court because they hadn't informed the police.'

The Music Society choir had its première at a concert in Croydon, Surrey, in June, 1971. In November, 1975, the Avalon Singers, a 45-strong choir from the south-east, made an appearance under the baton of Antony Hopkins at the Festival Hall's Purcell Room, with a programme ranging from the 16th-century Jacob Handl, through Holst and Britten to Antony Hopkins himself. Commending this range, the *Daily Telegraph* said, 'It is greatly to the credit of this choir that they were able to sustain the beauty of their tone and the interest of their audience throughout the programme.'

Another and more conventional WI skill was called into action only minutes before the performance when the conductor discovered that he did not have his concert trousers with him. A quick search revealed only one spare pair in the building, far too large around the waist. One of the singers lent him some dark slacks which, being a little long, were quickly tacked up to fit. No one noticed and the choir survived to perform, in January 1976, at one of the strangest concert halls in the kingdom – the former women's prison in the Old Gaol,

1952–53: Concern for a Queen

In 1952 the WI passed easily from concern for the pressures placed upon the young Queen who was, as the movement put it, 'a wife and mother' as well as a Queen, to the dangers of certain types of comics – see our pictures – which WI members felt were distinctly unfunny. This was an area in which the movement's campaign had considerable success.

THE QUEEN'S ENGAGEMENTS

An organization consisting mainly of mothers could be expected to sympathize with a young queen who was also a mother. Clearly the WI believed the Queen should be allowed to put family first.

Lodsworth WI, West Sussex, expressed the mood of the movement in a 1952 resolution which asked everyone to remember 'that our young Queen has duties as a wife and mother' and urged the nation not to overwork her.

The press gleefully took up the theme and it was also mentioned in Parliament. The WI may be said to have had something of an inside view on the Queen's problems, since she was a member of Sandringham, Norfolk, WI and attended meetings whenever she could do so.

RURAL ELECTRICITY

But at that same 1952 AGM the WI swiftly swung back to its first principles – concern for countryfolk – and Devon County Federation urged the government to speed up the provision of electricity in the countryside and to ensure that rural areas received a fair share of the capital available for electrification. Two years later West Sussex Federation pressed for a separate tariff for non-commercial uses such as village halls, educational establishments and charitable institutions.

By letters, memoranda and deputations the NFWI worked to implement both resolutions and in 1953 – together with other organizations – was instrumental in obtaining from the Southern Board a tariff concession which has substantially benefited Denman College as well as village halls and the like.

The NFWI, at the request of the government, regularly submits nominations for the Electricity Consultative Councils set up in 1947. A number of WI members serve on these Councils and on area committees.

WET BATTERIES

WI involvement in the life of the countryside got down to the small print of living – as a resolution demanding the removal of purchase tax on wireless batteries admirably demonstrated. Kinlet WI, Shropshire, put the resolution forward. Today it has an archaic ring but for people living in areas with no mains supply of electricity the wireness 'accumulator' was a vital piece of equipment. The National Federation badgered away at the chancellor of the exchequer and in 1953 the tax on wireless batteries was removed. Alas, in 1973 VAT swept through the land and wireless batteries became subject to the standard rate of ten per cent.

POST OFFICE SAVINGS

1952's resolutions showed the fund of practical good sense within the movement. Fulmodestone WI, Norfolk, believed that the £100 limit on Post Office Savings withdrawals without probate from a deceased person's account by those entitled to withdraw the cash was inadequate. They had to wait until 1965 for action, when the limit was raised to £500.

COMICS

The WI were also becoming concerned about the dangers of certain types of 'comics' which it felt were distinctly unfunny. Dorney WI, Buckinghamshire, urged all WI members who were the mothers of young families and all those who were responsible for the upbringing and education of the young to do their best to foster standards which would prevent their wishing to read such 'comics'.

'Progressives' may smile at the working of this resolution but events since 1952 tend to show that the natural, commonsense instinct of WI mothers was not so far off the mark. In the event, the Children and Young Persons (Harmful Publications) Act of 1955 made it illegal to print, publish or sell certain 'pictorial publications harmful to children and young persons'. The importing of horror comics was also forbidden. The penalty for breaking this law is a fine of £100 or four months' imprisonment – or both. Today, some may feel it is more honoured in the breach than the observance, depending on one's view of 'horror'.

EXPORT OF HORSES

Like all right-minded countrypeople – or right-minded townspeople, for that matter – the WI has always been concerned about the care and protection of animals. In 1955 there was a considerable public fuss about the conditions under which horses travelled from Eire to Belgium. But back in 1922 the WI had expressed its concern about the exportation of old horses in a resolution moved by Hatch End WI, Middlesex. In 1953 Topsham WI, Devon, sought the help of the Associated Country Women of the World and kindred organizations of women in all the continents to reduce the suffering of live horses in transit and at slaughterhouses.

That reference to 'all the continents' was a subtle touch since it demonstrated the sort of power the WI and its associates could muster in a worthwhile

international cause.

The resolution was sent to the ministers of food and agriculture, the Associated Countrywomen of the World and various animal welfare societies.

The NFWI also wrote to five Belgian women's organizations, one of which contacted the Belgian government which said, in effect, that in view of the recent rumpus more care would be taken in future.

There the matter rested until an incident at the end of 1959 in which some 50 horses perished on board the *SS City of Waterford* in a storm while being transported from Eire to the continent. The NFWI wrote to the prime minister of Eire and corresponded with the Irish Countrywomen's Association.

It was as a result of this incident that the government of Eire imposed stricter conditions on the export trade in live horses and finally, in 1965, banned the export of horses for slaughter. In Britain a number of orders have been made over the years which consolidated existing laws, extended them to air travel and provided for inspection for fitness to travel.

Abingdon, in Berkshire – a place one might have thought better suited to some macabre drama production.

Demand for good plays

Drama has enjoyed even more popularity in the villages than WI singing. An article in *Home and Country*, 1920 – the year of Pirandello's 'Six Characters in Search of an Author' – noted that 'one need not travel very far to discover that there is a great awakening of interest in the drama in this country. In many towns and in country villages too the demand is for plays – and for *good* plays.'

The editor of the magazine had already set an example with her own play, 'Britannia', which had a national success and was performed in many village WIs. For further encouragement, the National Federation issued a list of what were termed 'suitable' plays for WIs. Rather hastily, the WIs were cautioned that perhaps, after all, some of the plays were not *quite* so suitable. Meanwhile Miss Kelly started a Village Drama Society in the west of England and herself contributed regular articles on drama in *Home and Country* under the pseudonym of Greensleeves.

Just as Mr Leslie had initiated one day schools for village conductors, so in 1926 one day courses began for drama producers and, in the same year, there was a combined conference on drama and music. This activity culminated in a London Drama Festival in 1928, in which five WI teams performed at the Scala Theatre. There was a rather ambitious complete performance of 'The Taming of the Shrew', scenes from 'Julius Caesar' and outstanding performances by two ladies of over seventy, who had never been to London before.

Professional, amateur and WI

One reviewer called the Festival 'a daring idea'. Whether he liked it or not is hard to tell. Not so difficult to interpret were the comments of another reviewer after the second and far more daring Festival of 1933, in which men were included. The general standard of acting was, apparently, poor. 'The study of drama is the youngest and least developed of the WI activities,' said the critic drily: 'Until recently the standard was, with some isolated exceptions, deplorably low . . . In too many instances it has been regarded in WIs as a kind of ingenious game, a pastime, a little more elaborate than "General Post".'

Mr Miles Malleson, who adjudicated for the WI and once saw eighty one-act plays in five days, was a bit more reassuring. 'There is no need to be impatient if the movement does not produce geniuses and productions of great significance all at once,' he said. Perhaps, he argued, it should be remembered that in amateur theatricals only those with some experience of acting were usually included, whereas 'in an Institute we try to include every member, however inexperienced or ignorant, because we realize what a stimulus to the imagination and an unconscious education a study of this art can be.'

It was to no avail. Critics stuck to their own criteria. 'Kitchen comedies in local dialect,' said one, decrying not the dialect but the lack of any other kind of drama. There were three kinds of drama, said another wit, 'professional, amateur and WI'. There was only *one* kind of action the WI could take in the face of these jibes – persevere and enjoy themselves: the critics were not on their wavelength.

Working hard for nothing

Festivals of combined arts proved the best way to bring drama alive and in the early days the villages and counties excelled at pageants, which nicely combined song, dance and drama. In 1930, while Bernard Shaw's 'The Apple Cart' played on the London stage, Warwickshire presented a typical pageant in the grounds of Warwick Castle, featuring Ancient Britons, Roundheads and Cavaliers, Shakespeare and Press Gangs – each episode allocated to a particular section of the county to perform.

The pageant played for a week to packed houses and American visitors came flocking in their hundreds, 'not only to see the pageant, it was said, but in the hope of getting a glimpse of the lady who could persuade 5000 people to work hard for nothing'. Gwen Lally was the miracle worker and Bess Hughes the member who recalls that 'the final Hail to Shakespeare followed by "Jerusalem" sung in the twilight in the magnificent setting of the tree-ringed arena, with Warwick Castle and the Avon in the background, will always remain in my memory and rivals even the soul-stirring of "Jerusalem" in the Albert Hall.'

In 1951, Mr Attlee's Labour government deployed Herbert Morrison to arrange a demonstration of class unity and British solidarity: his conjuror's performance was the Festival of Britain. To everyone else it was a jamboree and the WI played their part whole-heartedly, with pageants throughout the country. Well stage-managed, yet at their most spontaneous, the WI enjoyed themselves just as evidently as their audience, which was a reasonable criterion for good value at any level of drama.

Robert Gittings wrote a cycle of five plays, called 'Out of This Wood', especially for the WI National Drama Festival of 1956, the year of John Osborne's 'Look Back in Anger'. And in 1961, a play-writing competition lured forth a whole new range of talent. There were 293 entries, of which 25 members had already had a play published or professionally performed. Other entrants had certain problems: 'My family are very kind but treat one's play-writing activities as one would a backward child – tolerantly but not generally mentioned in public.'

The next WI National Event will be a Drama Festival in 1980. Meanwhile WI drama holds its own in the forefront of the educational field. In particular, it has an outstanding reputation for training members in effective speaking. In 1976/77, the BBC is doing an educational programme based on this idea. Drama Certificates through the Drama Producers Training Scheme are accepted on a national level, outside the WI.

The sort of confidence gained from drama experience can also help WI members appearing increasingly on local radio. A number of County Federations have already been given regular spots to talk about the things that interest their members. Radio Birmingham presented an eleven week quiz programme between Warwickshire and Worcestershire Federations. Warwickshire were the winners.

One of the best-known ex-WI members in the theatre world is Joyce Grenfell, who was for a time president of her village WI in Buckinghamshire, which was instrumental in starting her career. At a cocktail party among friends she gave her own rendering of a WI speaker's talk on 'How to make something out of nothing'. Herbert Farjeon was among the delighted audience and he asked her to write her piece down and perform it in his show. That piece became one of her best-known monologues, 'Useful and Acceptable Gifts'.

Painting for pleasure

Members of the WI have shown gifts for other forms of art, as well. The Denman course on painting is extremely popular and, during the summer, artists can be seen dotted around the grounds happily hunched over their easels or stretching back to size up their subject. In 1963 there was a WI Academy at the Federation of British Artists Galleries, London. The title was 'Painting for Pleasure'.

A documentary film-maker produced a 'Painting for Leisure' film on painting in oils, which featured several 'Painting for Pleasure' exhibitors. A film has also been made on 'A Journey to Denman College'. Although the film covers many aspects of Denman activity, there is one notable exception – for a very good reason, as the director's wife remembers: 'We asked Donington WI in Leicestershire to come and do a country dance on the lawn for the film. Three car-loads drove a hundred miles at their own expense and when they arrived it was pouring with rain, so they had lunch and after lunch it was pouring with rain, so they had tea and after tea it was pouring with rain. At six o'clock they had to set off back to Leicestershire and that is why there is no country dancing in the Denman College film.'

Pageants, outdoor theatre, even Mr Leslie's mountaintop minstrels – rain can strike any of them and probably has done. But if the greasepaint runs, on face or canvas, the WI are not deterred. The philosophy of comradeship, in music, art or drama, overrides such petty setbacks. After sixty years, they know there'll be lots more opportunities.

A chance to learn

'GLADLY would he learn and gladly teach': Chaucer's Clerk of Oxenford gave to the WI a torch they kept bright to lighten work and play. Produce, crafts, music, drama – they could, where possible, hand on the old traditions; much better to blend these with new ideas and pass on professional advice. Household hints, home-cooking, child-care, health – even villagers whose old ways worked well needed help with new equipment, new standards, safer hygiene.

Six universities were opened in the first ten years of the century, examples of civic pride and the growth of higher education: not much help to village folk. If they wished to learn, they had to fight for teachers of their own, organize their own classes, bully the authorities to spare them grudgingly given books. Local authorities sat snugly in the towns and townsmen were well-known to think country life inferior to their own. They had no wish to give to the villages amenities that townfolk took for granted.

'Books for rural areas on the rates!' they exclaimed with horror at the proposal of a county library scheme. 'Waste of ratepayer's money.' In many counties, the only way that villagers got books was through the WI, who despite the authorities acted in handling distribution, collection and changing. These efforts helped in getting eighteen counties to adopt a rural library scheme in 1924.

Woman power

Parish and county councils thought WI members a tiresome body of women. They were quick to ask them to undertake jobs their male staff did not fancy, such as house-to-house visiting to collect names or information. But they were loath to pay extra staff to 'wander off into the countryside' and possibly get lost, an unending, nightmare drain on financial resources – with what return? The education of the villages? Ratepayers' money down the drain again!

In the 'wilds of north Bedfordshire' the village of Dean had experiences typical of many others. Their County Federation asked the county authority to appoint a domestic science instructress. The authority refused but offered instead a small grant. Welcome as that was, 'it was woman power we wanted'. So members with special skills took proficiency tests to supply the need themselves. In time, after continued pressure from the county chairman of the WI, who was herself on the county education committee, the county authority took one step back: they appointed an instructress but threatened that her services would immediately be withdrawn if not fully employed.

They felt they were on safe ground. How could she find enough to do among the villages? It was a generous gesture that would prove their point and save them further trouble and expense. She would cost them a month or two's salary at the most. To their amazement, she was overworked. The cost to the county trebled. A cookery and a craftwork teacher were appointed to assist her; later a horticultural teacher joined them. Those among the councillors who had thought the villages not bright enough to benefit from instruction found themselves besieged by the WI with absolute proof that villagers were as keen to learn as townspeople.

Mrs Mackay Brown was a VCO who worked with the WI in Bedfordshire. She feels sure that 'many people had little idea of the social and educational activities which were fostered in the 1920s by the WIs'. 'Fifty years ago,' she remembers, 'it was very difficult to make people

Denman College – a beautiful building in gracious grounds. This is a view of the College from the herb garden.

realize that though country life was different it was just as valuable as town life to the nation.' It became the self-imposed duty of the WI to prove the truth of that and, to that end, they co-operated with local authorities wherever those authorities could be persuaded to show any interest. If no interest was immediately forthcoming at once, they pressed for it.

The great network

At first there was a tendency among the village WIs to discuss a range of subjects at little depth. With the encouragement of Mrs Watt, for once in agreement with the National Federation, meetings began to explore particular discussions more fully. As members showed themselves prepared to look at topics in depth, the WI expressed its interest in acting as agents for local education authorities in bringing to the attention of the villages the educational facilities made available by the county council – such as classes which were open to the whole village. Mrs Jenkins points out in her history that it was through this agency that 'a great network of institute-sponsored village classes was spread over the English and Welsh countryside'.

By the extortion of county grants, by the appearance of WI members on county education committees, by the employment in council schools of certain members who had become expert in their fields, by bringing the needs of its members to the attention of such national organizations as the Adult Education Council, the WI generated an enormous amount of educational activity among the villages which benefited members and non-members alike.

A Board of Education White Paper of 1926 describes WI work, congratulates them on the teachers they had helped to train, commiserates with them over the problems they had encountered in finding places in which to hold their classes, commends the awareness that WIs had brought into village life and concludes that the results 'can only be regarded as phenomenal'.

'When you educate a man, you educate an individual; when you educate a woman, you educate a family.' Grace Hadow and Lady Denman both believed in this maxim. The Denman Report of 1928 was a major contribution to such education. Lady Denman's biographer, Gervas Huxley, recorded the concept, fundamental to the Report, that village women made a double contribution to agriculture: 'The independent contribution of women farmers and paid workers' (of whom there were over 100,000 in 1926) and 'the "co-operative" contribution made by a very much larger number of women and girls by virtue of their position as wives or daughters in village homes, where they are far more intimately associated with and have a far greater influence on the work of their menfolk than is the case in other industries.'

Lady Denman also sat for twenty years on a committee formed by the Ministry of Education for selecting boys and girls for Ministry of Agriculture scholarships. In a series of talks for country women, especially arranged by the BBC, she showed herself to be the leader of one of the country's largest pressure groups in an area where *everyone*, not just the WI could benefit. She reminded her audience that county councils had a duty to teach cooking to country girls and women, that they were failing in this duty and that it was consequently the duty of the WI to pressurize them into action. At the time of Lady Denman's speech, only one in three girls from country elementary schools received the required teaching and, in many counties, there were no classes

available at all for adult women.

Under Lady Denman's chairmanship, the WI fought and largely won their own battle, between the World Wars, to provide country women with professional teaching in country skills, by the appointment of rural domestic economy instructresses in every county. During this same period, the nation itself had largely neglected higher education. Very few universities were built in the 1930s; even school-age education was limited. Ramsay MacDonald's Labour government planned to raise the school leaving age to fifteen in 1931 but was defeated by the slump; in 1936 the National government under Baldwin tried again and failed; under Neville Chamberlain plans made to raise the age in 1939 were defeated by the war. The only bright point in these repeated frustrations was the increase in grammar school pupils from nearly 400,000 to nearly 550,000 between 1923 and 1938.

Their own university

The war was full of planning and preparation, highlighted by the Beveridge Report and Butler's Education Act of 1944, which at last raised the school leaving age to that elusive fifteen and proposed a complete national system of education. The WI caught the spirit of the time. They proposed their boldest plan to date. In 1946, they launched an Appeal for £60,000 to open their own College for adult education. It was to be named Denman College, in honour of their first chairman, who resigned that year.

'When we think about our WI College,' said the proposer of the motion at the Albert Hall, 'I want you to imagine a place that will be homely and welcoming, where in the pleasantest possible surroundings, away from the responsibilities and distractions of our usual lives, we can learn about useful, practical crafts and in addition where we can become better informed about the things going on in the world today, where we can learn more of our heritage and consider and discuss the future.'

Lady Brunner, who was one of the moving forces behind the creation of the College, is still closely involved with it. She had heard

WI members get down to action in a market gardening course at Denman College.

Sir Richard Livingstone talk about the Danish People's High School, went to have a look in Denmark and returned to search for premises in England. Marcham Park, near Abingdon, a late Georgian house with 100 acres, and taken over by the RAF during the war, came up for sale and was quickly bought for £17,000. The rest of the money went towards doing it up and preparing it for its new role.

The College was opened by Sir Richard Livingstone in 1948. County Federations contributed bedspreads, lampshades, even cushions, complete with regional designs and county emblems. Extra buildings were brought into use in co-operation with the Berkshire county council. Elizabeth Christmas was the first warden. Diffident about her own suitability for the job, alarmed at having to run a staff of forty, ill for much of her time as warden, she nevertheless managed to create a natural, warm and sympathetic atmosphere, where WI members, far from home, could relax and enjoy themselves – a tradition carried on by the present warden, Miss Helen Anderson.

A course at Denman quickly became one of the great experiences of life for thousands of country women. The house and grounds are beautiful and are kept superbly. It is a pleasure to spend a day there, walking by the lake, through the woods, across the lawns, catching sight and sound in light and spacious rooms of classes far too busy to take any notice of the passing visitor. Denman soon provided more than just an educational experience. Members could meet others from different parts of the country and compare notes. They could prove to themselves that it was possible, after all, to leave children and husbands for five days without catastrophe. They could return to their village WIs full of new ideas and information to pass on.

For some, it was the first time they had spent a night away from home. Denman was almost like going abroad, with all the excitement of novelty, all the reassurance of a home from home, a fund of stories and knowledge to accumulate. It was the best thing that had happened to the WI since the movement began and it was the final step in their independence.

Ripples in a pond

The first Denman course was very suitable: 'The Education of the Countrywoman through the WIs'. The second was a general course which is still one of the most popular on the list: 'Country Housewives'. Within ten years of the opening, a reporter from *Home and Country* dropped in on Denman and was able, on the same day, to see slides on Arctic exploration, a film about Leonardo da Vinci, a flower decoration class, a painting class in water colours and a talk on 'Science and ordinary people'. In one of the intervals, she heard the story of the woman who applied for Intermediate Patchwork and had to make do with Poetry because the class had been over-booked. No harm was done. She gained a whole new interest and enthused her family as well.

In 1976, Denman offered about 175 five-day and weekend courses on anything from painting to philosophy, lace-making to local government, from yoga to cathedrals, from book-binding to weather reporting, and including the world of the cinema, the environment, 'our multicultural society', the American bi-centenary, motorcar maintenance, 'the child in society', American music, Italian speaking and a wide range of more conventional WI interests such as drama, flower arranging and cooking. In 1977 archery joined the ever-growing list. 'A Denman course can be like a pebble thrown into a pond,' said one in-

Keep Britain Tidy – a national campaign sparked off by the WI, seen in action in our picture in the shape of a 'roadside patrol' displaying the latest litter tally. In its best rural manner the WI also took a keen interest in the campaign against foot and mouth disease.

KEEP BRITAIN TIDY

1954 saw one particularly memorable resolution – this time on the unpromising theme of litter. Northumberland Federation Executive Committee requested the NFWI Executive Committee to launch a campaign to prevent the desecration of the countryside by litter of all kinds.

Every member of the WI was urged to take up the campaign. Anti-litter laws should be more rigorously enforced! As far back as 1925 a Westmorland Federation resolution had drawn attention to the litter menace but after the 1954 resolution the WI swung into full action. Attempts were made to finance an anti-litter campaign but to no avail. The WI then decided to see what could be done with existing resources.

In March 1955 it was decided to form a Keep Britain Tidy group and more than twenty organizations, representing many different interests, signified their willingness to join.

In 1957 the WI asked the Ministry of Housing for grant-aid for the Group and the following year the housing minister agreed to a grant of up to £1500 a year for three years. This made it possible to appoint a full-time secretary, working in the NFWI offices. The Group became independent in 1961. The Queen Mother became patron of the Group and Lady Brunner succeeded the late Princess Royal as president in 1966. The Group has a council on which some 54 organization and firms are represented. In 1968 the Group was made officially responsible for the national campaign against litter. The annual grant from the government has continued to increase. It was fixed at £130,000 for 1972–73 and at £200,000 for the next two years subject to matching contributions from non-government sources. There are now about 7500 Keep Britain Tidy school committees and the Group has regional offices in the North West, North East, the Midlands and in Wales. Many WIs have co-operated in National Anti-litter weeks.

As the WI pointed out – few people realize what enormous sums are spent on the clearing up of litter – something in the region of £25,000,000 a year by the local authorities alone.

VIOLENCE IN THE PRESS

1954 also saw the recurrence of a theme which the WI had pressed before – the increasing tendency of some sections of the press to focus in detail on violence and lurid reports and pictures. These reports and pictures, said All Stretton WI, Shropshire, were 'of no interest to decent families and might do definite harm to the younger members of the family'. The resolution suggested that the best way of countering these excesses was simply to stop buying the newspapers concerned.

In this and in resolutions about many other social matters the WI simply put forward the common-sense views of ordinary people trying to bring up their families with decent, traditional attitudes. Sometimes society in its more avant garde manifestations appears to be doing its best to thwart their efforts.

SMALLPOX VACCINATIONS

From 1956 to 1960 the WI covered a wide variety of issues. Steyning WI, West Sussex, was concerned by the fact that not all children were being vaccinated in early infancy. It urged the Ministry of Health to publicize the necessity of early vaccination as a defence against smallpox and asked WI members to give every assistance.

The WI had been concerned with vaccination since an Oxfordshire Federation resolution of 1924.

TURNSTILES IN LAVATORIES

Turnstiles in women's public conveniences infuriated Littleham WI, Devon, and a great many others, too. A 1956 resolution sparked off a campaign against them. This has been largely successful but anomalies remain in some areas although local authorities were forbidden to instal them from 1963 onwards.

The sheer ordinariness of many of these resolutions passed by WI annual meetings is part of their attraction. Big national issues are, of course, important, but so are the thousand and one little things of life and it is these that authority and government tends to overlook. Perhaps a 'parliament of women' – as the WI has often been described – would add a touch of common sense to legislation.

PURCHASE TAX

Again, the WI tried to inject a touch of logic into the zany and quite arbitrary workings of the purchase tax regulations. Spondon WI, Derbyshire, pointed out in 1957 that whereas many men's working tools did *not* carry purchase tax, kitchen utensils, including electrical appliances, did. But weren't cooking utensils a tool of the housewife's trade?

This resolution duly went off to the chancellor of the exchequer and two years later – in 1959 – joint representations were made to his successor. Although cuts were made in the tax over the years, the 1973 VAT regulations put the usual ten per cent on. Subsequently, the WI have protested at the inequality of VAT impositions. Why should housewives be regarded as second-class working citizens?

water supplies and sewage facilities in country districts. In 1958 Southerndown WI, Glamorganshire, returned to the attack. Immediate practical action was urged to improve all inadequate sewerage systems, as a prime essential of public health in the country as much as the towns.

FOOT AND MOUTH

Foot and mouth disease was the theme of a Rattery WI, Devon, resolution of 1959 which asked the minister of agriculture to give nationwide publicity to the risk of spreading foot and mouth disease by the indiscriminate disposal of uncooked bone and offal.

A good, practical point. In 1968 the NFWI sent a memorandum to the Northumberland Committee of Inquiry into the disease, based on evidence supplied by the County Federations. The Committee published its report in 1969 and in that year the foot and mouth regulations were revised and strengthened.

MODERNIZATION OF COTTAGES

The wholesale destruction of old cottages which could easily be modernized was another WI theme. In 1958 Westmorland Federation Council asked the housing minister to urge housing authorities to consider the possibilities of repairing old cottages before demolishing them. The Housing Act of 1969 did much to help since it made provision for improvement grants.

SEWERAGE FACILITIES

Resolutions of 1928, 1930, 1934, 1937 and 1943 had already stressed the importance of good

A judging course at Denman College in the 1950s. Mrs M. J. Dunn, Produce Organizer, is by the door.

vigorated pupil, 'the water ruffled extends in a wide area and so, too, are the thoughts stirred and stimulated . . .

In the first four years, there were an average of 1500 students a year at courses at the College; now more than 4000 attend each year and many more apply. More than half these come to Denman for the first time and during the summer months another 3000 come as day-visitors. Husbands can also come to stay – and learn – when their wives attend a course, though there are limitations of space. By the time Denman celebrated its Silver Jubilee in 1973, nearly 65,000 students had taken courses at the College. For each of them, it was a chance to enjoy the leisure of education without the hurdles of exams; for some, who had turned away from the competition of learning, it was a chance to have another go.

Each looked for and received something a little different, from the early member 'who took no part in discussion but sang lustily and often wrongly and seemed to enjoy things' to the lady from Leicester who studied Elizabethan England and made newspaper headlines when she mentioned in a subsequent talk that Elizabethan women wore no knickers. 'When one hasn't attended any classes for over thirty years, it's quite an adventure to start again,' said one student.

An artist considered that 'five glorious days at Denman with a wonderful instructress taught me more about painting than I would have muddled through in five years at art school'. She had just received her highest commission – 300 dollars for a portrait to help her pay her fare back to England from Australia. Another student felt that, by attending courses on architecture, she had been able to speak out more intelligently at enquiries on local development and contribute a little 'to saving apparently insignificant period houses from being demolished in favour of horrors such as petrol stations'.

Pass on the word

Facilities at Denman have been expanded over the years and members have worked hard to contribute to the cost of their own College. It was hoped that the original £60,000 would be raised in three years; in fact it took five years to raise and the Carnegie Trust contributed another £20,000. A new bedroom block was added in the grounds with the help of an anonymous donation and the WIs themselves contributed £30,000 during the 1960 Denman College Year. In 1970, new accommodation and teaching blocks were opened, mainly financed from the 1965 National Appeal Fund, during which £500,000 was raised.

Finance is a great problem, both for the College and for WI members. If a member has never experienced the benefits of the College, it is easy to become alienated by the apparent expense and it is hard for those not involved to realize the high costs of running a large country house with all the services that it provides. The cost of travel to the College does not help. Courses are not expensive but many members cannot afford to go. Therefore Denman relies for support on the good publicity it receives from past students. 'Pass on the word,' said Grace Hadow, who did not live to see the College: she meant, pass on what has been learnt; she could equally have meant, pass on the news, it's worth a visit.

Similar financial problems apply in local areas, where education authorities are cutting down on their activities because of cost, while transport becomes increasingly difficult. Once again, as in the beginning, the WI are accepting responsibility to apply pressure where needed and, where pressure can have no effect, 'gladly to teach' as they would 'gladly learn' themselves.

Mrs Hoodless maintained that education was the root of democracy. Discussing the Education Bill of 1944 and warning that 'the chance of an education bill may not come again for another twenty or thirty years', the parliamentary secretary to the Board of Education congratulated the WIs on the 'valuable report' they had made in answer to a questionnaire issued by the Board on the subject of the forthcoming Bill. 'A first class piece of reporting,' he called it and concluded, 'You are now the most active workshops of democracy.'

Books
and sport

Other aspects of WI willingness to teach itself are the range of publications and the sporting activities. Besides basic literature about the WI and reports on village conditions to government departments, there have been many booklets on crafts and produce. In 1958, the best-selling 'Wines, Spirits and Cordials' sold 60,000 copies in four years, closely followed by 'Yeast Cookery'. 'Homemade Wines' is still one of the best-sellers but you can also buy not-so-closely guarded WI secrets on Lotions

and Potions, Hedgerow Baskets, Continental Quilts, Picture Framing, Wood Sculpture, a book of carols, Tie-dye and Batik, Toy Patterns, Herbs and Spices, and Unusual Preserves, including parsley honey and Cumberland bean salad – if that takes your fancy.

The counties have also published a lot of material. Many of these are valuable collections of memorabilia, such as Norfolk's 'Within Living Memory', and local recipes. There are, too, Cornish walks, Essex embroidered smocks, Guernsey patterns, Herefordshire poems, Hertfordshire 'Women at War' and roses, Lancashire Lore, Warwickshire oil painting and a book from Northamptonshire called 'Going Crackers', which is not about a psychiatric unit but about making crackers.

After the war, several village WIs, such as Spelsbury and Burford-and-Fulbrook, produced records of the wartime experience of their whole village. These accounts are fascinating to read. They reflect a strange phase of social life and leave the reader in no doubt how, by common sense, they managed to survive. The WI is particularly well-placed and well-equipped to make this sort of record.

Records of another kind are now being made in sport. Cricket teams were put into the field early in WI history. They were smartly turned out with all the proper gear and performed with considerable skill. Tennis is now one of the most popular sports, encouraged by an NFWI/Green Shield Stamps Tennis Championship for which, in 1976, there were 606 pairs entered from 44 counties.

Most sport is carried on at county level: a Lancashire Swimming Gala and bowls championship; a York badminton championship; a Norwich Swimming Survival Day; a Cornish evening gala with badminton, table tennis, trampoline, yoga, weights, archery and squash. There are also regional sports conferences and, in 1977, for the first time, a Sports' Leaders Course at Denman College.

True to WI traditions of giving help wherever possible, County Federations responded to a request for comments from the Home Office's Working Party on Water Safety in 1975. A healthy mind in a healthy body: who better than the country women to know the importance of keeping fit and to go about it in a wise and balanced manner.

Bridging the gaps

IT is not enough for a healthy democracy to educate itself. That is only the first step. Country women did well to demand instruction in practical and pleasant activities but to become responsible citizens they had also to turn their education to the help of others. In their Golden Jubilee Year, they resolved 'to increase their efforts to serve the community'. 'It seems to me,' said the Queen Mother, 'that members are in a position to be of help in just the human and personal way in which no official service can hope to do.'

This was nothing new. They had, through their resolutions, shown their responsibility since the beginning; they had expressed their concern through *Home and Country*; they had acted directly wherever they saw a need. Through individual help and collective pressure, they turned their resources to best advantage, to help the unemployed, to fight for better housing, to establish the rights of women, to promote better health and better public transport, to stop accidents, to counter crime, to improve the environment.

As a woman's organization, their concern to establish the rights of women was understandable. While rejoicing in the new woman's vote after the First World War, they came face to face with the ugly awareness that, after the slaughter, the country then possessed two million 'surplus women' – an awkward political mote that everyone wished to forget.

Surplus women

Not so the WI, who could hardly avoid it. The Lady Isobel Margesson tried to reassure them. True, she said, their chances of marriage and motherhood were decreased and the necessity for economic independence was *increased* but their value to the state depended purely on their efficiency. *All* efficient citizens, she said, of both sexes are an asset to a nation. In any case, the so-called surplus was a splendid argument for better training, better openings and equal pay for equal work. What employer could now complain that women were not worth their salary on the old excuse that they would leave to marry!

There was, concluded Lady Isobel, a 'wonderful change in public opinion which now recognizes the claims of women to the duties and responsibilities of citizenship, for which they must thank the pioneers of Women's Emancipation, 'upon whose foresight the members of the WI could build'.

Other correspondents to *Home and Country* took another view. It had been proposed that women should be encouraged to emigrate and join selected husbands in Australia, where there was by contrast a male surplus. These men were to pay weekly contributions to a suitable society which would arrange the marriage. There was an outrage. 'Are women to be mated like prize animals!' exclaimed one correspondent. 'And not even in accordance with the principles of eugenics?'

Another took the idea more calmly: 'If, having approached the Colonial Office (for the safety of girls) you are successful in arranging an intelligent co-operation of both sides, viz. the men in the colonies and the women in England, will you kindly put my name down as a candidate (middle-aged but not wholly unattractive) for New Zealand. I am prepared to buy a money box and put aside the sum of 2d (tuppence) a week toward the fare.'

Determined to be heard

Meanwhile, if women were to be in the majority, then they were determined that their voices

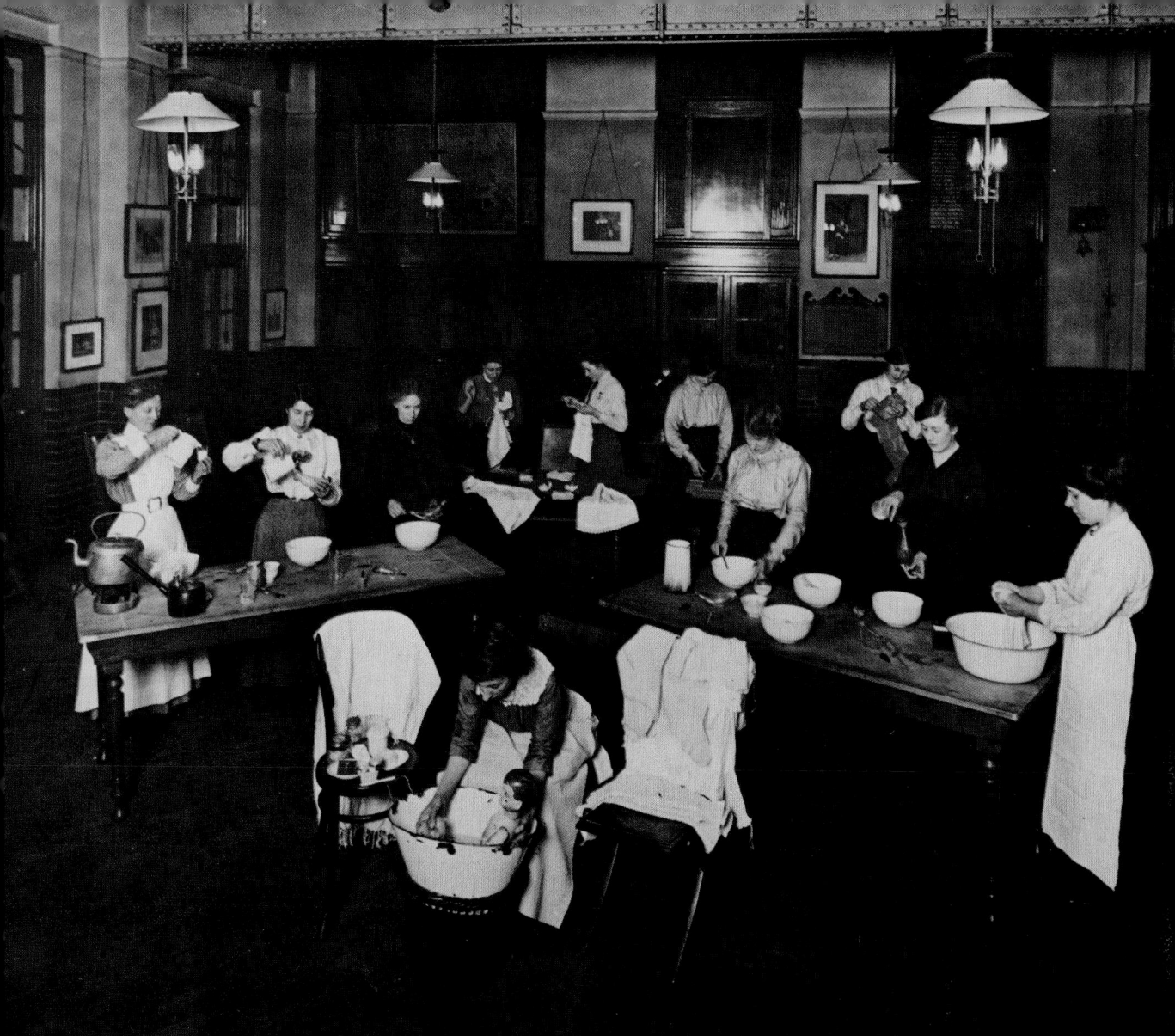

Young women – not WI members – being instructed in baby care in 1915. The WI promoted this idea.

should be heard. From general elections to local elections, they were exhorted to use their vote. Use it wisely, they were cautioned and, wherever there is a suitable female candidate, use your vote to help her to a position where she can further the interests of women. The WI responded nationally and locally. In 1919, Lady Astor became the first woman member of Parliament to take her seat. In subsequent local elections, WI members themselves penetrated the indignant fortresses of local councils.

Home and Country set the pace with an article whose title, 'The Science of Government' was taken from Johnson's definition of politics: 'WIs have not sprung up all over our country districts without awakening the members to a sense of responsibility in many ways

undreamed of before,' began the writer. 'Women all over England find themselves responsible for the government and well-being of their country ... and most are ready to acknowledge that they are wholly unfit, through ignorance, for this great responsibility. To confess ignorance and to be conscious of unfitness for responsibility is to proclaim oneself a willing pupil.'

The pupils learnt fast. By the end of the year (1921) they were pressing for women members on parish and district councils, for they claimed that women in positions of such responsibility would give 'a more complete effect to the democratic process of self-government'. 'Question and Answer' columns

Bridging the gaps

in *Home and Country* kept interest alive and the members well-informed of the complexities of local government, their rights, and the opportunities available to them.

In 1937, *all* parish councillors were to retire. It was an excellent chance for women to gain a stronger foothold. 'Do nowt and pay nowt' was the economic philosophy fondly held by male councillors but known to be false by women who understood the need for safe playgrounds and who felt the strain of drawing water from the well and the inconvenience of boiling it. The rates for mains water connection might be high but, as one Lancashire member said bitterly, 'We spend more than 't rate i' buckets.'

If the odds seemed against them, prospective candidates were urged not to despair. They were reminded of the Yorkshire woman who had sought election to her parish council a few years earlier. She had obtained *one* vote and everyone had laughed. Not in the least upset, she proposed a vote of thanks to the chairman, since none of the men had bothered to do so. She was returned at the next election.

Wives and mothers

The rights of women to speak their mind in government were coupled with their rights as citizens, wives and mothers. In 1921, they demanded the right to sit on juries; forty years later, they insisted that the qualifications for jury service were outdated. At the same time, they were fully prepared to face the penalties of their own misdeeds: in 1922, they passed a resolution in which they stated 'that a law which allows a woman to shelter behind her husband in wrongdoing or crime is now obsolete'.

They welcomed A. P. Herbert's Matrimonial Causes Act of 1938, which gave a wife equal rights to divorce and some chance to replan her life. In 1920, they gave strong support to the government's Bastardy Bill which, some years later and in another form, made legitimate a child whose parents subsequently married.

Much later they were quite prepared to question themselves on a fundamental point: 'Does a child gain by being born in the country?' Despite the majority of arguments in favour, the answer was not a foregone conclusion. Infants in isolated districts were not always able to benefit from welfare centres.

Out of work

These few examples reveal an inborn concern for their own sex. Their concern for the problems of the opposite sex was equally apparent from the beginning and revealed a practical understanding that the problems of both sexes were closely linked. Unemployment was an evil that threatened the whole family with starvation and misery.

The outcome of the General Strike may have been a personal triumph for Prime Minister Baldwin but it was a tragedy for the miners, a tragedy from which they found it hard to recover. The TUC rejected the strike when the miners refused to accept the government's revised terms, and the miners remained off work alone for another six months. When they returned to work, it was on the mine owners' terms. There was little mercy. The Depression hit them when they were already depressed.

There were almost 50,000 miners and their families in need of resettlement in 1929 – *if* the miner himself could be persuaded to leave the coalfield. An appeal went out to the villages: Could they find work for one more man? Was there not, somewhere, a deserted cottage that would serve for accommodation? Work of almost any type was sought. There were carpenters and smiths from the surface as well as face workers.

The National Council of Social Services approached the WI to help in realizing the aim of 'one village, one family'. This, they said, would be the biggest single contribution yet made to a solution of the problem – a far more constructive task than immediate financial relief. The National Council assured the WI and other organizations in the village that it would, of course, take the utmost care in selecting suitable families and would bear all the costs of transporting the family. Just how such 'suitable' families were to be chosen was left unmentioned.

The village WIs were cautious. Many had troubles enough of their own: there was barely enough work in the village for the villagers themselves. Others felt able to help a little. Two Durham mining families were given work in Sussex; a Devon village engaged a miner as an assistant electrician-chauffeur; a Yorkshire village arranged farm work in six-week shifts on different farms for a miner on the look out for accommodation for his family.

This was the other side of the problem: where there was sometimes work, there was often no room for the whole family. Lack of housing proved a greater obstacle than lack of work. Agricultural workers were themselves looking for jobs and there were already long waiting lists in the villages for new housing.

Even so, work and homes were found: foundry work in Essex, sewage work in Surrey, farm work in Cornwall, quarry work in Hampshire, work for a mason's labourer in Devon and for a mechanic in another part of Essex, and (a busman's holiday) mining work in Kent. In one Surrey village, a mining area itself, work was found for a jobbing gardener and the WI found accommodation and encouraged his family to come down, agreeing to guarantee a proportion of the rent.

Help was a concern of the whole village, as in the Devonshire seaside village of Thurlestone, where fifty miners working on the golf course were made welcome by villagers and in many cases housed and helped with clothes by WI members and others. Parcels were also sent to their families and some of the men were able to find permanent work in the neighbourhood.

In 1937 the condition of the miners had improved only a little. Aneurin Bevan wrote about their working life and exhorted the women in the mining districts (among whom were many keen WI members) to bring pressure to bear on the authorities to speed up the installation of such amenities as pithead baths, than which 'no single amenity means more to the miner and certainly to his wife'.

The right to a roof

The WI experience with the miners in 1929 had reminded them how close were the problems of unemployment and housing. They had fought to have their say in housing since 1920, when they chalked up a notable victory over Wimborne and Cranborne Rural District Council

The council wrote to one WI member, announcing that they had 'considered applications made to them by various branches of the WI in their district for the appointment of at least one woman upon their Housing Committee and have accordingly appointed you as a member of this Committee'.

They followed with interest the criticisms of Neville Chamberlain's 'rabbit hutches' and the Labour Housing Acts of 1924 and 1930. The housing boom of the 1930s did a great deal to alleviate unemployment for it provided work for many ancilliary trades, such as carpenters and furniture-makers, but by 1938 unemployment was once again building up toward figures characteristic of a slump.

In that year, the WI were reassured by the minister of health that help was available to local authorities in the provision of adequate and satisfactory houses for workers on the land. The Housing Act of 1938 was intended to 'open a new era in agricultural housing'. 'You need not be alarmed as to the effect of this programme on the rates,' beamed the minister; subsidies were available.

Subsidies were never enough. Hardly surprising, therefore, that the WI started doing something about housing for themselves. One of their most useful and enterprising schemes was started recently by Warwickshire Federation. Seven members supplied the necessary money to register a housing association and invited three professional advisers to join their committee. The local authority lent £33,000 as a mortgage to purchase a house, which was converted into thirteen flats.

The house was large, rambling and old but stood in its own grounds and was structurally sound. The tenants are either widows or retired single women. One of the tenants acts as warden, and the local WI bring their husbands along to help keep the garden in order, while they themselves use their own skills to decorate lampshades and rooms. Rents help to pay off the loan, interest payments, rates and maintenance but the flats are run on a nonprofit basis. Anyone can join the association for a fee of one pound and a waiting list quickly built up which justified a second house.

Such an association is not unique but the WI are themselves in a unique position to be able to organize such a project and, to give it a

Traditionally the WI has been interested in family health. In 1960 they pointed out the startling fact that four out of five children entering school in Britain had some form of tooth decay. Noise, too, was beginning to disturb even remote rural areas. The WI campaigned against the supersonic flights of civil aircraft over Britain.

DENTAL CARE

The WI believes that the dental condition of people in this country leaves much to be desired. By the time children enter school four out of five have some decayed teeth – largely due to the nation's passion for sweets and confectionery. A 1960 resolution from Much Hadham WI, Hertfordshire, referred to a resolution of 1926 drawing attention to the problem and urged that more widespread instruction on the prevention of tooth decay should be given and that the importance of diet should be stressed in ante and post natal clinics, in schools, WIs and other institutions.

UNNECESSARY NOISE

Noise – or rather unnecessary noise – was the theme of a 1960 resolution from Heamoor WI, Cornwall, and of a subsequent campaign. The WI decided to support the anti-noise campaign and a resolution was sent to various government ministries, motoring organizations, the metropolitan police, the BBC, the TV Programme Companies and the local authority associations.

In October 1960, a memorandum containing evidence from County Federations and individual members was sent to the Government Committee on the Problem of Noise and in December of that year Mrs Jacob (now the WI Chairman) led an NFWI deputation which was interviewed by the Committee. In 1967 the WI sent comments to the Ministry of Transport about draft regulations to control motor vehicle noise and in 1968 letters were written to the ministries concerned urging that supersonic civil flights over Britain should not be allowed.

A number of County Federations also sent comments in 1973 to the Department of the Environment about proposed legislation on noise abatement.

ROAD SAFETY

Road safety in the countryside was also very much a matter of concern to the WI. An East Sussex Federation Executive Committee resolution of 1960 expressed grave concern over the increase of road casualties in the countryside and the WI pledged itself to do everything possible to help solve the problem. The movement is represented on the National Road Safety Women's Section of RoSPA. WI members have also trained as instructors for child cyclists. Again, this demonstrates that the WI does not simply pass resolutions – but acts, as well.

VIOLENCE ON FILMS AND T.V.

The 1960's were a busy decade for the WI. There was still concern about violence on films and television as a Stapehill WI, Dorset, resolution of 1961 demonstrates. The WI pledged itself to do all in its power to arouse public opinion to an awareness of the detrimental effect this had on children and young people.

FREEDOM FROM HUNGER

Cornwall Federation Executive Committee put forward a resolution (1961) pledging the NFWI to support the Five-Year Freedom from Hunger Campaign. The movement played its part in the educational campaign in this country by helping to provide speakers and collecting £185,000 to support various

projects. They provided scholarships, study courses for women leaders, rehabilitated a fishing fleet in Ceylon, provided bulls and a rotovator for Tristan da Cunha, bought £11,000 worth of trained buffaloes for Sarawak, and provided the cash to support either wholly or in part many other campaign projects.

DANGER OF FIREWORKS

In 1962 Llanddaniel WI, Anglesey, took a tilt at the dangers of fireworks and bonfires and urged that the retail sale of fireworks should be banned until a fortnight before November 5. Little progress has been made. In 1963 the manufacturers agreed to discontinue the making of the cheaper 'bangers' and it was also agreed that bangers of any description should either have plastic caps or be sold in boxes. In 1976 the government said sales would be banned until three weeks before November 5. Progress indeed!

COUNTRY HOSPITALS

The closing of small hospitals in country districts was deplored in a Langham and Barleythorpe WI

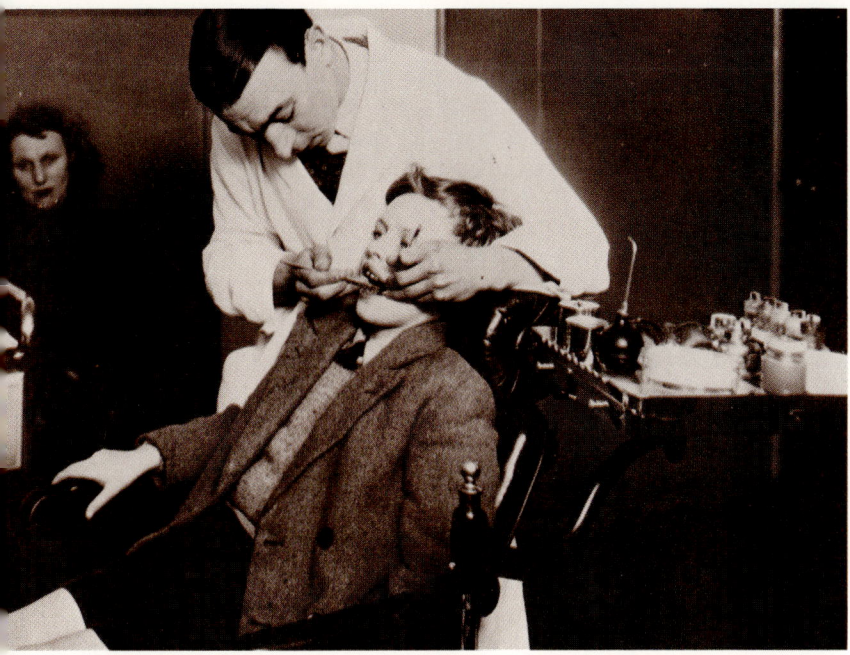

(Leicester and Rutland) resolution of 1963 and the movement launched a campaign.

Breconshire Federation Council in 1964 invited the government to accelerate the development of alternative sources of water supply and made the progressive and sensible suggestion that distillation of sea water should be tried. It was. In 1970 a pilot desalination plant was installed at Ipswich in Suffolk but the scheme was abandoned in 1972.

DIVORCE REFORM

The WI was also concerned about the Divorce Reform Bill and in 1968 Three Stones WI, Essex, put forward a resolution insisting that the Bill should include provisions granting a deserted wife, whose marriage has been terminated, financial security, tax reliefs and the pension rights of a married woman.

This Bill failed to complete its passage through Parliament and in 1969 a Divorce Reform Act was introduced but although this introduced two new grounds for divorce — by consent after being apart for two years, and after five years even if one partner objected — no definite principle for the award of maintenance payments or allowances for tax relief and pension rights were enacted. In 1971 the WI submitted evidence to the official committee on One-Parent Families.

DRUG ADDICTION

Greys WI, Oxfordshire, introduced a resolution in 1966 urging parents and those responsible for children and young people to make themselves aware of 'the very grave danger in the easy availability of habit-forming drugs and drugs of addiction'.

Letters were written to the home secretary and various other government departments and departments and organizations. A number of Counties held conferences on the subject and in 1969 the movement published its own leaflet entitled 'Parents, Children and Drug Abuse', which has had a wide circulation both inside and outside the movement.

sense of internal continuity by maintaining interest in the welfare of the tenants without imposing sectarian benevolences on them.

The ultimate
authority on milk

The rights of women, the right to work, the right to a roof – just as important was the right to good health. Baby shows were only a beginning. From a resolution on venereal disease in 1922 to a resolution on compulsory free family planning in 1972, from the health of children to railway hygiene, from cervical cancer to village surgeries, the WI presented their case for reform.

In 1922, WIs were urged by *Home and Country* to help in maternity and child welfare schemes. This they could do by helping to establish a good district nursing association, by helping the midwife in her work, by establishing welfare centres and by setting an example to the village in the storing of food.

The minister of health spoke to them again in 1938: 'Good health, in my judgment, is not to be measured only by the wane of disease or the postponement of death,' he said. 'Good health at its best should give an active joy in life.' To that end, he asked for the assistance of the WI in making known to country districts the facilities that the forthcoming National Health Service intended to supply. He urged them to bring to his attention any problems with regard to such amenities as water supplies and the provision of adequate milk. Ten years later, with the National Health Service newly formed, they were approached to disseminate propaganda on its behalf.

This did not stop them being critical. They had pressed for increased consumption of milk for years. In 1934, the minister had answered their resolution, demanding cleaner milk, with an unfortunate turn of phrase, as Miss Marshall remembers: 'Glancing round the packed audience of women, he brought his talk to a close by exclaiming, "After all, you women, you are the ultimate authority on the production of milk." We were all more polite, or perhaps more inhibited then, but a suppressed titter went round all the circles of the Albert Hall and the poor man blushed to the roots of his hair.'

Nutrition and milk went hand in hand. In the same year, Professor Mottram urged the WIs to still greater efforts. 'The dieticians want you to consume milk and milk products,' he wrote. 'Isn't it time you women pushed Parliament into doing something about it?' On November 8, Lady Denman herself gave a BBC broadcast, explaining to the WI how they could best help to bring this vital problem of nutrition to the attention of country people.

The subject appeared again in Lady Denman's address at the 1938 AGM. She begged the WIs to write to their members of Parliament lobbying for the provision of cheap milk, and she promised that such a concerted effort *would* be listened to. 'One Member of Parliament,' she said, 'suggested that he would have been saved a lot of trouble if he had received one letter from the County Federation rather than fifty from individual women's institutes. I suggested in reply that it was always possible for one letter to be overlooked, whereas fifty were bound to receive attention.'

In reply to her speech, the minister referred to 'the immense service that the Women's Institute movement has rendered to the life of our countryside, how it has laboured during the 22 years of its existence to raise the standards of living in the countryside.'

Caring
for the sick

The minister was not the only one to appeal to the WI for help. In 1951, the consultant physician at St Bartholomew's Hospital, London, said that 25,000 people were cured of cancer each year, representing only half the number that might be cured if the fears of the other half could be overcome. Education was necessary, he said, to enable them to recognize the early symptoms which might make it possible for cures to be effected.

'Women's Institutes,' he concluded, 'have a unique and unrivalled opportunity to help in Cancer Education by organizing lectures and distributing pamphlets, thus doing away with Fear and Ignorance, obtaining early diagnosis and saving thousands of lives.' In the words of Emerson, which Adelaide Hoodless had no doubt known by heart, 'Knowledge is the antidote to fear.'

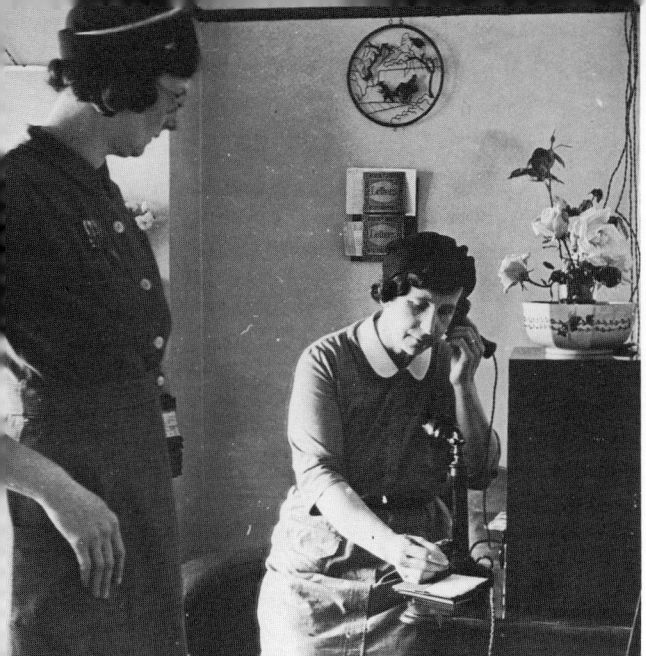

The WI fought for a village midwifery service.

Only a year before, another kind of fear had been recognized – the fear of small children in hospital, separated from their parents for the first time. The WI passed a resolution insisting on the importance of parental visits. This was at a time when the general public were only just beginning to realize the harm that such separation could cause. The discussion at the AGM was widely reported and greatly influenced public opinion. But it was another ten years – ten years of continued pressure – before the need for such visits was wholly accepted. By that time, the WI were discussing 'Mother and Child' units, in which mothers could sleep in the hospital with their children. Once again, they were in the forefront of reform.

Concern about hospitals was not only in relation to children. In 1931, the WI pressed for patients to be allowed to sleep until a reasonable time in the morning if it was not absolutely necessary to wake them. In consequence, several hospitals modified their habits. This aspect of hospital routine was still being considered in 1971.

The movement has also been interested in the welfare of the mentally sick for many years. It was Cambridgeshire Federation, who formed an experimental WI within a psychiatric hospital. There are now over sixty WIs in psychiatric and geriatric hospitals as well as in Cheshire Homes. These 'Special WIs' are often started at the instigation of the hospital itself. Not only do the meetings form a focal point of interest inside the hospital but, when

patients leave, the WI members are able to keep in touch with them and help to rehabilitate them by introducing them to WIs in the neighbourhood to which they go. Such integration is considered of great help and importance by the hospital.

'Day Hospitals' and Day Centres are another concern – WIs pressed for their establishment, 'to enable older members of the family to share the home without undue hardship and stress for the younger generation.' In such units patients and the elderly can spend a day of varied activity and interest under care and a watchful eye. The mandate on a matter such as this, like many others, is sent to the appropriate Ministry to encourage action. It also helps to inform WI members themselves on subjects of which they might not have heard before. In deciding how to instruct their delegate to the Albert Hall ordinary women are better informed on several new questions and can pass on their knowledge to their fellow members. National Federation literature is available to reinforce this new awareness and to provide background information.

Country midwives

Some resolutions are fashionable, some anticipate fashion, some will never be fashionable. These last are no less important. Nutrition was fashionable in the 1930s, when the WI discussed it; midwives were not and possibly will never be.

Hard-working, hard-pressed, the midwife was officially licensed to practise in 1902 and became a well-known figure in the village. It was not her fault that the service she could provide was often limited by the extent of her training. The WIs showed particular interest in the Midwives Bill of 1936, which aimed 'to improve the standard of domiciliary midwifery in England and Wales by establishing an adequate service of salaried midwives.'

After the war, the WIs heartily endorsed the decision – long sought by their members – of the Central Midwives Board that all pupil midwives were to take a course in the administration of gas and air analgesia for childbirth *before* enrolling as midwives. Many had never taken this course at all because to do so

Bridging the gaps

had hitherto meant taking two weeks off work, which was impossible when there was no adequate temporary substitute midwife to take their place.

Analgesia was another step forward in the struggle to obtain for the country woman the right of painless childbirth. Further correspondence in *Home and Country* discussed the possibilities of self-administration, as much to provide psychological courage as physical relief. As a result of WI pressure, gas and air machines for analgesia were widely distributed in country districts during the 1950s.

Equally unfashionable was the performance of the last offices for the dead. In 1950, the WI published a pamphlet called 'Your Village', which gave a detailed picture of the rural communities of England and Wales. Facilities were fully charted: buildings, village halls, post offices and telephones, junior schools, bus services, water and sewerage, electricity, midwives, surgeries and provision for the last offices for the dead. It was a comprehensive survey. From a total of nearly 12,000 civil parishes and villages, nearly 7000 WIs replied to the questionnaire: one WI often represented more than one village – so almost every village was surveyed.

Asked which of these services the WI felt was most wanting in their village, Rudgwick, in West Sussex, claimed their greatest problem was the absence of anyone to perform the last offices. One hopes the summer was not hot. In Radnor, the superintendent of nurses gave talks on the subject to the WI.

Churchyard surgery

Other villages felt the lack of country surgeries. Some produced interesting solutions to the old problem. Parishioners and WI members in one Devon village furnished a consulting and waiting room in the old church vestry. In warm weather, the patients preferred to sit outside on an old pew among the gravestones – not the liveliest of company for those in need of good cheer and healthy encouragement!

Inadequate transport makes it even more difficult to reach what surgeries there are. In East Sussex, 'people have to beg lifts from neighbours or while away hours waiting for

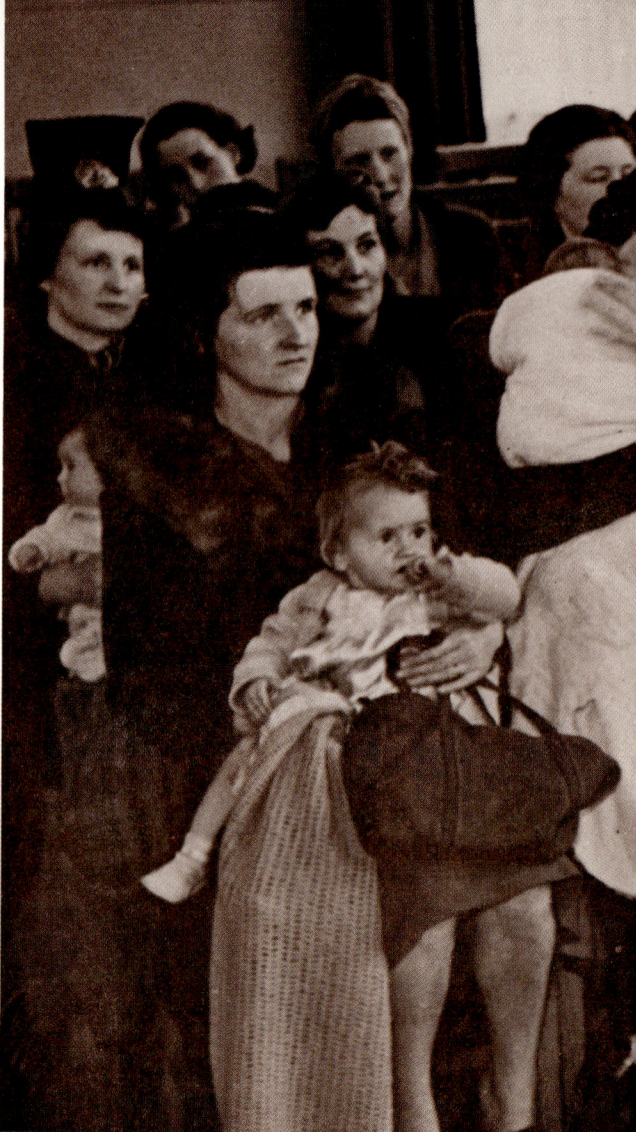

Maternity and child welfare schemes were advocated by the

infrequent buses, or even walk several miles to get medical attention. The carless section of the community – the elderly, the women with babies – are often least able to stand up to effort of this kind.' The WI expressed its opinion forcefully that if health centres were to replace branch surgeries, then a central authority should work out a satisfactory transport system. Meanwhile voluntary help is the only practical answer to the problem – convenient for government since no one has to pay the volunteers for anything.

Great Tew, in Oxfordshire, concerned lest lifts given by members to country people should be construed by bus companies as competition, thus providing those companies with an excuse to withdraw out of pique what services they did run, suggested that surgeries

WI from its earliest days. This picture was taken at an early Birmingham welfare centre.

should be held in private houses in the village. This would enable the doctor to make an efficient round of several villages in a single morning. In Skillington, a surgery has been held in the front room of a private house for seventy years. In Thornton, Leicestershire, the Bricklayers Arms opens its smoke room twice a week to local villagers to come and consult their doctor. Until recently, the same pub also housed the WI infant clinic.

Two years' nagging and perseverance in a Cornish village, where members adopted their president's slogan, 'never take "no" for an answer and never give up putting your case', won for them from their county council a portable building for a surgery next to the WI hall, which the WI also use as a baby clinic. In Rutland, one doctor makes use of two spare

bedrooms and a rented cottage in three successive villages, carrying with him simple drugs and his patients' medical cards so that he can follow their case histories. 'It might be obviously more efficient to have a central surgery from the administrative point of view,' the doctor said, 'but this set-up is far more appreciated by the people themselves.'

Many general practitioners are not so sure it is a good idea to have local surgeries, where there are not the facilities to handle the more difficult cases at once. They add that patients must still visit the chemist in a nearby town to obtain their prescription. Barnack village has the answer to that. WI members help out with a Red Cross scheme to provide volunteer drivers to get patients to their doctor. To prevent abuse of the service, the doctor gets in

Bridging the gaps

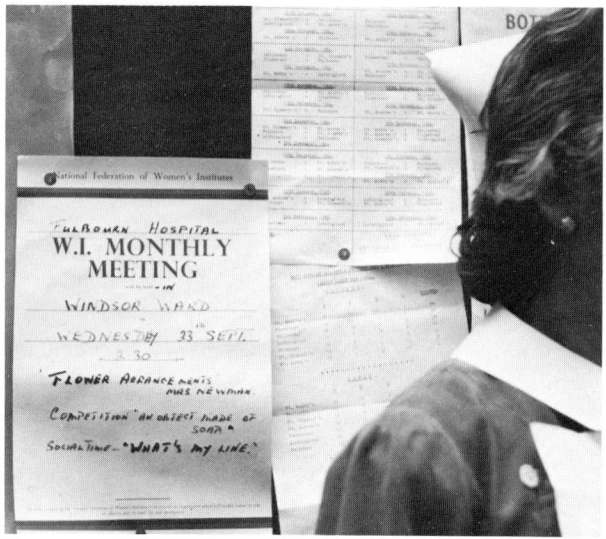

Even hospitals have their institutes. This notice on a hospital board advertises all the usual WI attractions.

touch with the volunteers when he hears that a patient wants to see him. In turn, the volunteers also provide a prescription delivery service, with an evening run for emergency prescriptions.

Transport
without accident

In Cheriton Fitzpaine, Devon, where there had been no bus service for eighteen months, WI members presented the results of a village questionnaire on transport needs to the county council. A bus was arranged to run to the nearest town, Crediton, twice on one day a week, on the condition that fares covered at least half the running costs. Four months trial was what the council offered. Nearly two years later, the bus service is still going well.

The problems of transport – for shopping or doctor – led naturally to those of noise and accidents – both severe health hazards! A memorandum was sent to the Ministry in 1960, based on evidence collected from WI discussions and by a direct random sample of members from thirty counties. Mrs Jacob laid emphasis on excess noise at night, noise from motor cycles, car rallies, aircraft noise. Seven counties complained of aircraft noise. Complaints were also made about round-the-clock noise from dairies – just to prove the WI were

impartial judges between town and country. The memorandum coincided with the Noise Abatement Act that came into force in November 1960.

'Stop Accidents Year' recorded the Golden Jubilee of the Royal Society for the Prevention of Accidents, in 1966. WIs read the available literature on everyday dangers such as driving, fireguards, medicine cupboards, re-wiring, slippery mats. One in 200 people was killed or seriously injured in preventable accidents each year. 'We must recognize and accept that accidents don't "just happen",' said the Duke of Edinburgh, opening the campaign. 'Every single one of them has a cause and reason and every single one of them could have been prevented.' Prevention began, as the WI well knew, with teaching children to be careful. Who better to teach them than their mothers? As ever, the WI were not satisfied with one year's campaigning: in 1968 they turned their attention to the dangers of farm accidents.

Crime and
the courts

Though mothers might try to influence their children for good, there were plenty of bad influences which concerned the WI. In 1970, the British Medical Association commended the WI leaflet on 'Parents, Children and Drug Abuse'. It was suggested that, with doctors' consent, copies of the leaflet should be bought by County Federations and placed in doctors' waiting rooms.

In 1921, the WI passed a resolution demanding an official Board of Censors and in 1948 they insisted on tighter controls to prevent their children being exposed to the more harmful cinema programmes. Brought up on innocuous British comics, in 1952 the WI condemned the proliferation of the American style, with its 'vivid portrayal of cruel and sadistic acts, of murder and torture'.

In 1922, along with a bill curtailing seditious teaching to the young, Parliament passed the Criminal Law Amendments Bill, in which the government acted with surprising promptness 'on account of the great demand from women's organizations of every kind that the "age of consent" should be raised and the safety of children and young girls (and boys) be provided for far more adequately'. The 'age of consent' was once more the subject of debate in 1976, when it appeared as an urgency resolution at the WI annual general meeting in response to an announcement by the home secretary that the Criminal Law Revision Committee was to undertake a comprehensive review of sexual offences.

Family Courts have been the subject of discussion in the 1970s. The WI was asked, should these courts, dealing with matrimonial, maintenance and property problems, become part of the welfare state? A questionnaire published in *Home and Country* was based on the Law Commission's paper on Family Courts and the findings of the questionnaire were sent to the Commission. In the true tradition of the WI, it was felt that, should the Family Courts be made part of any new social welfare organization intended to provide all necessary family services, there would be a serious danger that party politics would 'affect, through committees, judicial functions which should remain independent'.

More recently, the WI have ensured that they are fully informed on all aspects of crime and punishment. In 1974, they invited four

Mrs Penny Bardwell speaks out to 5000 fellow delegates on membership subscription rules at the 1976 annual general meeting.

eminent speakers to air their views at a WI Conference in London. The speakers were the chief constable of Devon and Cornwall, the chief probation officer, the permanent under-secretary of state at the Home Office and the 'Angry Brigade' judge, Lord Justice James.

Current concerns

With representatives from the Department of Health, the Home Office, the Department of Prices and Consumer Protection and an expert on pensions all on the Public Affairs sub-committee of the WI, the committee is able to take advice and in turn advise members on almost every aspect of day-to-day living. Whether it is a problem of electricity or pensions, hire purchase or leases, legal aid or sex discrimination, the WI have the resources to inform themselves of the most up-to-date legislation, to help others, to speak out with intelligent concern and to be, as the chairman of the committee puts it, a 'powerhouse for action'.

In 1975 their resolutions were on familiar themes: screening for breast cancer, battered wives, national insurance benefits, equality of opportunity, amendment of the law with regard to rape and a pledge to intensify WI education in the production and preparation of food in view of the universal shortage of resources – one of their founding concerns. In 1976, their first problem was to safeguard their own financial security: that done, rabies, the Rent Act, VAT, rural transport and the 'age of consent' were all subjects for debate at the Albert Hall.

National resolutions and mandates are not always immediately successful in obtaining government action. Often local members are thrown back on to their own resources in an emergency, as was the village of Fakenham, Norfolk, which took issue with the turnstiles in its public lavatory. Other villages had also complained of similar difficulties. A national resolution was passed but government action was slow. Fakenham WI wrote to the parish council, calling the turnstile 'an indignity to all women ... It presents real difficulties to mothers with young children, to the aged, the infirm, the outsized, and to all women encum-

Countrywomen are always on the alert – whatever the problem! The WI thinks nothing of tackling badgers, juggernauts and crafts in one AGM afternoon. The juggernauts, alas, and their invasion of our villages and historic towns, are still with us. But the WI were among the first to sound a warning.

SUPPORT FOR CRAFTS

In 1970 the WI moved back on to tried and familiar ground – the importance of crafts. The NFWI Executive Committee asked the government to support crafts on a scale comparable to its support of the arts in general. This was felt to be vital in an increasingly mechanized and leisured society.

Letters were sent off to the appropriate ministers and informal discussions took place with the director of the Craft Council and representatives were appointed to that Council and to the World Crafts Council.

JUGGERNAUTS

That contemporary abomination the 'juggernaut' was a subject of WI wrath in 1970 when Barrowby WI, Kesteven, expressed the movement's objection to proposals to increase the permitted size and weight of commercial vehicles. Fortunately, the government agreed with the WI. At an interview with Peter Walker, then the Secretary of State for the Environment, the NFWI representatives welcomed the government's decision to keep to current size and weight restrictions and to ensure that foreign lorries conformed to these.

BADGERS

Badgers, those most genial of country creatures, also caused the WI some concern in 1970. Willaston-in-Wirral WI, Cheshire, asked for legislation to prohibit the killing of badgers except by special licence. In 1973 The Badgers' Act made the killing of badgers a punishable offence except by authorization.

INLAND WATERWAYS

Inland waterways form part of Britain's scenic charm and, suggested Aldenham WI, Hertfordshire, in a 1972 resolution, the government should provide more cash for their restoration and maintenance, particularly in view of the increasing public interest in water-based recreations.

In August 1973 the government duly announced that the Water Space Amenity Commission would advise on recreational policy for all inland water space and would also take a look at capital schemes for the provision of recreational facilities.

RURAL TRANSPORT

In the last few years mandates have been approved on many new public issues as well as issues that the WI have kept alive for years. The needs for an adequate public transport system, for example, have always been important to the country people who rely on it so heavily. In 1973, the National Federation urged the government to formulate a comprehensive transport policy and demanded a closer look at the disparity in expenditure on roads and railways.

This concern was followed up in October, 1973, by a letter to the minister of transport, welcoming his efforts to encourage the transfer of freight from road to rail. But this did not solve the problems of local transport in rural areas. In 1976, a mandate was approved which demanded greater flexibility in rural transport schemes. What was required, said the movers of the resolution, was for the law to be amended so that private schemes could be set in motion where public schemes were inadequate.

TRANSPORTATION OF ANIMALS

As a rural organization, the WI were also well-placed to understand the dangers involved in transporting live animals. In support of the 1973 mandate urging the government to ensure that all animals exported for food should first be slaughtered in the United Kingdom, letters were sent to the minister of agriculture, the National Farmers' Union and to animal welfare societies. A memorandum was also sent to the Committee of Inquiry into Export of Live Animals for Slaughter under the chairmanship of Lord O'Brien.

A free vote in Parliament on the

issue concluded with the lifting of the ban on live exports. But the failure of the WI in this particular provided an excellent example of their determination to pursue their humanitarian aims to the best of their ability in the prevailing conditions. A letter was sent to the minister welcoming the additional safeguards which had been imposed and expressing the hope that everything possible would be done to encourage the eventual substitution of a carcase trade for the trade in live animals.

FREE FAMILY PLANNING

In support of earlier mandates, the WI were active during 1973 in pressing for a free family planning service. Letters were exchanged with Sir Keith Joseph on the subject. A request was also put to Sir Keith that WIs should be given the opportunity of putting forward nominations for the Community Health Councils when these were set up. Follow-up information on the reorganized National Health Service was sent to the counties the next year. Publicity was also given to a new leaflet published by the Women's National Cancer Control Campaign. The leaflet provided answers to many of the questions asked by those who had never hitherto taken the cervical cancer test.

RURAL PLANNING

Planning has always been of high priority in the WI and much of their value and efficiency has been the result of good planning. In 1973, they recalled their post-war planning of the 1940s by disseminating information on future Structure Plans at local and government level. Planning to preserve the countryside and planning against pollution also featured in their 1973 campaigns.

bered with shopping bags and baskets.' A second letter claimed 'it is narrow and can cause congestion on Thursdays'. The offending turnstile was removed. It was another victory for common sense and the WI.

Keep Britain Tidy

Some of the concerns that have been mentioned properly belong not so much to public affairs, where the 'gaps in society' are most obvious, but to environment and agriculture, for which the WI have a separate sub-committee. The concern of that committee is for a different kind of gap but one which nonetheless divides society – the gap between those who care for the countryside and those who expect it to take care of itself. Those 1930s hikers, we came across earlier, had much for which to thank the work of the WI. This committee also has Ministry representatives. Its aim is 'constantly to seek up-to-date information, with the help of those representatives, on planning, transport, pollution, water supplies, pest controls, toxic chemicals, quality control on foods and so on'.

Transport problems, noise, rabies – these all affect the conditions of the countryside in which people have to live. Easy enough for townsfolk to think they are the only ones who have problems with noise and transport; easier still for them to forget that an outbreak of rabies can kill not only their own pets but themselves as well – a single lap-dog smuggled in by a thoughtless tourist could, without the owner knowing, cause a national epidemic.

Litter is probably the cause for greatest conflict between town and country, though rusting eyesores and plastic fertilizer bags can be blamed on country farmers too. 'High minded Institute members prowling the commons with pointed sticks,' remembered that there was strength in numbers. 'Pull in the Scouts and Guides,' they were told, 'who are knowledgable, athletic and not at all afraid of smells.'

In the mid-twenties, they asked the minister of health to urge local authorities to provide facilities for collecting rubbish. Two years later they took a stand against unsightly hoardings for advertisements. In 1928, mem-

bers of Shere WI began their own campaign, 'not to drop litter, to remove if possible any they see and to prevent others from spoiling the countryside'. Chelford members assumed the name of 'Pug Pups' and did the same.

These activities culminated in the formation of the Keep Britain Tidy Campaign in 1955, of which the WI were among the chief founders. Aesthetics were not the only issue. Bottles and tins left in fields after picnics often injured animals, and litter thrown into crops could damage expensive agricultural equipment. The National Federation helped to organize all forms of publicity – press, TV, posters and speakers – to keep alive the nationwide campaign.

Support was given to the Anti-Litter Bill which, for the first time in the history of the country, made it an offence to scatter litter in any public place in Britain. The 'Minister Against Litter' congratulated the WI. 'If before long,' he concluded, 'we can bring public opinion to hate litter as it hates squalor and disease, it lies within our reach to create conditions in which the whole country will look back with disgust and astonishment at its indifference only a few years back.'

There was a children's poster competition. The winning poster showed a sow with four piglets and a Keep Britain Tidy bin in one corner. The caption, in bright, bold lettering, challenged: 'SHE TAKES CARE OF HER LITTER – WHY DON'T YOU?' This was joined in 1967 by the Nursery Knight poster, showing a cheerful looking knight on the back of a rocking horse, tilting his lance down at the ground to pick up litter. The National Anti-Litter Week which he led was an attempt to educate 'that youthful sweet-wrapper dropper who becomes the adult cigarette-end and packet fiend – not to mention old-furniture and broken-down-car abandoner'. 'No Litter' was the slogan for the following year and in March 1976 a week was devoted to Project Spikey.

Scrapbooks of the Countryside

There was strong support, the year after the war, for National Parks, a concept in which Britain lagged far behind Canada and the United States. In 1927, a resolution was passed

Northamptonshire WI members collecting litter.

against pollution at sea from waste oil thrown over by ships. A later resolution urged the minister to improve sewerage and clear the seashore of pollution.

The WI called a Conference on the Country-side, at which Mrs Jacob noted that 'Nature can cause havoc. Man, indifferent and apa-thetic, can cause even greater havoc.' Members told of successes achieved by local pressure groups: an important stretch of harbour mouth saved for migrant birds in West Sussex; detailed pilot surveys made of the counties of Warwickshire and Somerset; tree preservation orders won in Lancashire; a Yorkshire protest against the erection of pylons, which had earned the congratulations of a visiting inspector.

In European Conservation Year, 1970, WI members preserved more trees, cleared foot-paths and old watering troughs, made a survey of Devon field names and, in Devon, too, helped raise money to buy a stretch of coast land for the National Trust. They joined in the AA Plant-a-Tree drive. In their Jubilee Year, they compiled their own 'Scrapbooks of the Coun-tryside' and received encouragement from the minister of agriculture: 'May your important work in environmental and other fields go from strength to strength,' he said.

Author Paul Jennings based a book on the countryside scrapbooks, which he called *The Living Village*. The scrapbooks, he said, had 'an immediate, unarguable sense of reality' and contained 'a powerful sense of living in two times, in an old and a new Britain, with an awareness, an agility in effortlessly leaping from one to the other'.

In 1972, the fruits of another national WI event ripened. 'This Green and Pleasant Land' was a competition aimed to focus attention on the dangers to the countryside from pollution, pesticides, development and industry. Members could show a fifteen-minute 8-mm film, a programme of transparencies with a record or tape, a tape recording only, or an exhibit. Launching the competition, Mrs Jacob said, 'Although for 55 years we've worked to im-prove the conditions of the countryside, now we must *hurry*. We can't afford to be slow . . . Let's make thousands know what we're doing, positively, to conserve the countryside.'

European Architectural Heritage was the theme of 1975. 'Spying out the hidden treasures of architecture in towns and villages and making efforts to preserve them is yet another WI way of life,' said an article in *Home and Country*. In the same issue, there was a report on the success of an adventurous 'Town and Country Project', set up jointly by the WI and its old friend, the Carnegie United Kingdom Trust, in 1970. As the dividing line became increasingly difficult to define, the project aimed to establish links and understanding between town and country people. With com-ments from two boys such as, 'I thought milk grew in bottles', reminiscent of the experiences of evacuation in 1939, it was a project that had been overlong delayed.

Water resources, the recycling of waste, structure plans for the future of the country-side, conferences on the use and abuse of land – country care also concerned animals: hu-mane killers, export of live animals for slaughter, intensive rearing of livestock and even open-air zoos. The WI showed particular interest in 1930 in the London Zoological Society and the new zoos at Blackpool and Oxford, where 'animals could be seen in their natural surroundings'.

Members were well aware, in all their activities, that what they contributed was only a part of the effort by all concerned people. They had plenty of reason to be proud of their contribution but if, at times, they seem to take things personally, then they do so without intention. 'Blackpool,' it was reported, 'with its usual enterprise, is to make an open-air jungle. But it is unlikely, however,' said the article, with great apology, 'that this wonder-ful zoo will be ready in time for the WI annual meeting.'

A world to share

ONLY months before the outbreak of war in 1939, when the conflict was already inevitable and nations were racing to rearm with bullets, tanks and guns, country women from all over the world gathered in London for an international conference. Many people, including Lady Denman, were sceptical of the value of the meeting. It was Mrs Watt whose determined, stubborn will carried it through – a magnificent gesture of solidarity in the face of insanity.

The conference was held at Earl's Court. There were several functions to be attended and it was hard to know what to wear for each of them. The Norwegian representatives – one hundred of them – wore national costume all the time, so they had no worries. Anyway, it didn't really matter. All eyes were on the German.

She was clearly nervous and needed courage to address the meeting. Her organization had been banned by Hitler some years before. She spoke about very ordinary things, the daily difficulties of country folk that everyone could understand. They all listened with sympathy, agreement or curiosity at varied customs. It helped to define for all of them what they would be fighting for – a future in which they could meet again and discuss once more just such common pleasures and problems.

When she had finished, it was hardly surprising she received the loudest and longest ovation of the day. Turning to leave the conference, she said to Nancy Tennant, 'I've admired you so much but what I've admired most is your freedom.' Then, after that brief respite, she returned to her own problems.

Born in a time of war, the WI spent the interwar years deeply concerned with maintaining international peace. Like millions of others, they put their faith in the League of Nations, which exemplified their own belief that discussion could smooth any path. A League of Nations Union was created to organize and inform the public as to the work of the League and, in 1919, the WI was represented on the Woman's Committee of the Union and helped to obtain speakers from the Union to address local WIs.

About 600 WIs became 'study associates' of the League. 'There is no better way in which members of village institutes can help to ensure the future peace of the world than by learning to understand the League of Nations,' they were told with optimism. They could hardly be blamed for not realizing how false was this hope.

The League proved itself a lost cause, long before its members recognized its hollowness. Japan invaded. Manchuria in 1931 and the League did nothing. In 1934, for the second time, the WI formally pledged its faith in the League. In February they sent a delegate to the International Peace Congress in Brussels, 'In Defence of Peace', at which twenty countries were represented. The previous month, the president of the Disarmament Conference in Geneva wrote to the WI general secretary, Frances Farrer, thanking her for her 'urgent message on the subject of Disarmament' and exhorting the WI 'to continue with greater energy than before, to urge upon governments and public opinion the necessity for pressing on with our work for disarmament until success shall be achieved'.

Later that year, the Conference was disbanded. Hitler became *Reichsführer* on the death of President Hindenburg and carried out a purge of his followers on the 'Night of the Long Knives'. In England, Mosley's blackshirts provoked a violent meeting at Olympia and the Reverend Dick Shepherd founded the Peace Pledge Union. The Soviet Union was admitted to membership of the League of

The WI is a movement with world wide associations. These women are members of a housecraft training centre in Ceylon.

Nations – and all it stood for. It was a time when the deep-rooted fears of war made prevalent a fanatical belief in pacifism, a mood in which the WI wholeheartedly shared. Later, when Baldwin admitted that he had foreseen the danger to come and yet had declined to seek an election on re-armament, he was accused with vehemence of betrayal. Had he gone to the country at that time, he replied, a government would have been returned so emphatically pacifist that Britain would have been even less prepared for war when it came.

In 1935, a conference on international affairs was held by the WI for representatives of County Federations. In succeeding years, *Home and Country* contained articles to inform members on the annexation of Austria, the news from Italy, the Czechoslovakia crisis,

Russia, Turkey and the persecution of the Jews. A second conference on international work provided a demonstration on how to discuss international affairs without being controversial! Lady Denman emphasized that members should not shirk the difficult task of discussion whilst keeping to their non-party-political, non-sectarian rule. Seeming to anticipate some of the arguments produced on the amendment to the rule in 1971, she said, 'I believe we shall limit ourselves to trivialities and so do irreparable harm to our movement' if the WI did not tackle such discussion.

Lady Denman was less keen on the international interests of the WI than on agriculture, which was her particular field. From 1929 to 1939, she combined the two by sending a WI representative to the annual meetings of the International Commission of Agriculture, to which the WI became affiliated. The WI also became a member of the Women's Section of the International Congress of Agriculture and likewise sent representatives to biennial meetings. Papers were read by WI representatives to the Women's Section on 'Feeding a Rural Family', 'The Health of the English Village' and 'Rural Hygiene'. The WI only withdrew its membership to the Congress in 1948.

The aftermath of war

When war broke, links were kept with organizations in other countries through the sane counsel of Grace Hadow and, after she died, through Nancy Tennant and her International Committee secretary, Marjorie Freeman. Visits were arranged to Europe. Even the French wrote to say they were interested in starting a WI. Later, Nancy Tennant went to discuss the possibilities and quickly realized how very unsuited the French character was to WI-type meetings.

Support for the Help Holland Council was a major project towards the end of the war. Clothes, boots and shoes, blankets and household equipment were all needed. In particular, help was provided to refit the returning 'slave labourers' from Germany, who came, often penniless and in rags, to find their homes had either vanished or been stripped bare. People in long queues waited patiently outside warehouses for clothing and bedding. This was the urgent work of rehabilitation close to the heart of the WI, who knitted something like a quarter of a million garments for Europe and ensured the practicality of what they provided by consulting representatives of the recently occupied countries. Personal pen-friendships with overseas country women and help from sister organizations in America bolstered WI wartime morale.

Contacts with Germany were immediately reopened when war came to an end. Helena Deneke was invited by the Allied Control Commission to visit Germany and to advise on adult education and the welfare of German countrywomen in the British zone. She reported on the appalling living conditions in Germany, made worse by as many as two million refugees – women, children and old people – who were pouring in from the new Poland. One of Miss Deneke's duties was to try to revive the *Landfrauenvereine*, the country women's organization disbanded by Hitler in 1933. To that end the WI co-operated in making arrangements for four German women to visit Britain the following year in order to see women's work in this country.

It was not altogether an easy visit, as Miss Tennant remembers. The German women described conditions in their country, bombed, defeated and overrun. It was found necessary to remind them that Britain, too, had been bombed and was short of supplies. After that showdown, everyone got on much better. Problems remained, however, at local level. In 1946, Chidham still felt strongly about the Germans and a talk on 'Life in Europe Today' was cancelled because the speaker was a German. It was reported that there had been 'a very disturbed meeting at nearby Westbourne owing to the speaker's point of view'.

Ten more German women came for a three weeks' tour in 1948. Other parties followed, some of which published opinions of their visits. They were impressed by the democratic nature of the WI and the submission of resolutions to Parliament. But they were amazed to see husbands washing up dishes, dogs drinking tea and the 'superficial' or 'trifling' nature of local WI lectures on holiday trips. They found fun and games at local meetings most unnatural and decided that the fancy needlework they saw 'proved that the women of the WI must have much more time than we have'.

Visitors from overseas have always been welcomed by the WI, who co-operate with the British Council and the London School of Economics to arrange individual and party visits to national headquarters and to villages. Some visitors pass on their way to international meetings; others are studying social science or local government, or else are students at one of several international schools of English.

'International days' are a feature of many

local WIs, with all the colour of national costume and talks by those who have been lucky enough to go abroad. Wives of American officers serving in Britain have been coerced into talking about their home country. Hundreds of WIs have paired themselves with villages all over the globe, exchanging letters and gifts, interesting themselves in the welfare of their 'twin'. In 1954, a resolution was passed encouraging the 'promotion of international understanding among country women'.

Ambassadors abroad

The traffic is two-way. WI members on holiday abroad often stop to meet fellow members and bring home news. After Miss Hadow's death, a special Grace Hadow Fund was started to finance visits abroad by WI members. Local WIs sometimes finance their own overseas 'outings'.

At national level, Miss Deneke's visit to Germany was only one of several VIP visits. The Ministry of Information sent Elizabeth Christmas, Denman's first warden, on a twelve-week tour of Canada at the end of the war and in 1950 the Imperial Relations Trust financed visits by two other WI members to Canada, Australia and New Zealand. In the following year, the Australian government invited Lady Albemarle to attend part of the jubilee celebrations of the foundation of its federated government, the Commonwealth of Australia. No doubt they remembered Lady Denman's connection with their country.

Shortly before her death and with typical adventurous spirit, Grace Hadow took time off from walking trips through the wilder parts of Albania and Montenegro to accept an official invitation to go on a Commonwealth tour of 30,000 miles. She received the invitation on the spur of the moment, over the telephone, at breakfast – and accepted on the spot.

The visit that Mrs Pike paid to Russia in 1962 was equally adventurous. The invitation came unprompted and wholly unexpected directly from the Soviet Union in a telegram congratulating the WI on their Golden Jubilee. One hundred and fifty WI members applied for the job of interpreter. She visited Moscow, Leningrad and the Ukraine and her return was greeted by a press conference and an interview for BBC radio and television programmes.

Mrs Pike broke through Soviet bureaucracy and found the Russians friendly, easily amused and religious. She spent two days going round factories, before she managed to obtain an invitation to a private house in the country. 'I am interested in country women,' she stated firmly, 'I don't want to look at factories.'

International goodwill

It was at national level that the first discussions took place over the possibilities of an international organization of country women. Mrs Watt was behind the proposal and Lady Denman had reservations. WIs had already been spreading around the world: in New Zealand, Rhodesia, Australia, South Africa, Zululand and Ceylon – even in Bengal where, by 1928, there were 149 'Mahila Samitis'. As the movement spread, Mrs Watt became increasingly determined to bring together all these WIs into one body of women. Her early attempts were frustrated by the independent spirit of the different organizations.

Mrs Watt persisted. A little demoralized, she adopted an air of diffidence but snatched at an opportune suggestion by Lady Aberdeen that rural women should be represented on the International Council for Women. Lady Aberdeen was president of the Council and the wife of a former governor-general of Canada. Delegates from several country women's organizations met in London in 1929, under the auspices of the Council, to discuss their common interests. A liaison committee met the following year and an International Conference of Women's Institutes was held in Antwerp.

All this led to the formation of the Associated Country Women of the World (ACWW) in Stockholm in 1933. The chairman was Mrs Watt, who retained the post for fourteen years, until the year before her death. Such was the enthusiasm of delegates at Stockholm that two of them, a little over-stout, embraced each other so warmly that they lost their balance and fell from the platform. They received applause but no injury.

A topic is discussed in every WI before it becomes a WI mandate. The press may sometimes wonder how so many subjects can be dealt with adequately at one AGM. But every resolution discussed has been thoroughly researched. The AGM is the culmination of months of patient work and careful study. A good deal of hard thinking has taken place beneath those often derided hats . . .

In 1974 the movement urged a national policy to coordinate and develop the reclamation, re-cycling and re-use of ingredients in domestic and industrial waste. (Chobham Evening WI, Surrey).

RURAL RATES

The problem of rural rates was already worrying country people and High Ham (Somerset) WI urged the government to re-instate the Variable Domestic Rate Relief System throughout England and Wales in view of the 'enormous and totally unjustifiable increase with which ratepayers in rural areas are now faced'.

The protest was effective, too, for the government later announced a scheme for refunding 60 per cent of the excess to any ratepayer whose total rates and water charges had increased more than 20 per cent compared with the previous year.

County Federations have been asked to send in comments and suggestions to the NFWI on alternative ways of providing finance for local government.

EQUALITY OF OPPORTUNITY

In 1975 – in case there had ever been any doubt about the matter! – the WI nailed its colours firmly to the progressive mast in an NFWI Executive Committee resolution which declared, quite simply: 'The NFWI believes in the principle of equality of opportunity and of legal status for men and women and pledges itself to work to achieve this.'

BREAST CANCER CLINICS

And – once again a demonstration of the ease with which the WI can move from the general sublime to the important particular – the movement, through a resolution moved by Willoughby Waterleys WI (Leicestershire and Rutland), urged the government to set up clinics where any woman could be screened for breast cancer.

BATTERED WIVES AND RAPE

The AGM was also concerned about battered wives and urged immediate action for the provision of alternative accommodation for these women and their children 'at least in every county if not in every town'. This was moved by Barnack (Cambridgeshire) WI.

The movement also supported, in a Farnham (Essex) resolution, the Sexual Offences (Amendment) Bill asking for changes in the law relating to rape.

NATIONAL INSURANCE

But the WI is not, as we have pointed out, only concerned with resolutions of grand principle. It is a great believer in the day of small things – and of spotlighting everyday situations that can become problems for many people.

For instance, Cambridgeshire Federation urged that 'all persons who look after elderly or handicapped dependants should be credited with Class I National Insurance contributions in order that their retirement pension is not reduced by the fact that they have not been in contributory employment'.

The problem of the 'stay-at-home' daughter who sacrifices years of her life to take care of an ailing mother has been with us for generations. The WI, quite rightly, thinks this should be changed.

PREPARING FOR THE AGM

To those commentators accustomed to thematic conferences spread over several days, the staccato style of a WI annual meeting in which several subjects can easily be dispatched in a day comes as something of a shock. But this is a question of time and style rather than a lack of depth or basic research. Every WI resolution turned into a 'mandate' by the voting sanction of the AGM has been the subject of a good deal of thought and patient exploration.

For instance, the 1976 AGM tackled in one brisk day the need for more flexibility in transport schemes in rural areas, legislation affecting the availability of rented accommodation, the control of rabies, VAT on domestic appliances, the age of consent for sexual intercourse and a change in the Federation's rules concerning the annual subscription.

Much of the importance and value of these and every other resolution brought before the AGM is educational. It is in the preliminary exploration of the resolution brought before the AGM that the ordinary member becomes aware of the problem – an awareness that broadens her outlook on life whether or not the resolution is passed and regardless of the short time available for discussion at the AGM itself. Commentators on the WI who find the transition from theme to apparently unrelated theme at the AGM a little too swift to take seriously need to remember that the AGM is only the all-too-brief summation of a far wider and deeper educational programme.

Left: Jean Lewis from Essex proposes a resolution on rabies. Above: Rochford WI members make sure that, when rural transport schemes prove inadequate, they can keep their own cars on the road.

FOLLOWING THE MANDATES

The 1976 clutch of resolutions were followed up in typical WI style — letters to the home secretary, the Criminal Law Revision Committee and the National Council for Civil Liberties in the case of the age of consent resolution, letters to the chancellor of the exchequer and the Electrical Association for Women in the case of VAT on domestic appliances, a spate of letters to many bodies on rabies control, letters to government and county councils and others on rural transport services and more letters on rented residential accommodation. This is the WI pressure system at work. This book is a demonstration of how effective that can be.

A world to share

ACWW shortly became the largest women's rural organization in the world. Lady Denman pleaded commitments to the Congress of Agriculture and regarded the Association a little doubtfully, although it was London that hosted the 1939 triennial conference at which the German representative spoke out so bravely. Mrs Watt's hospitality stretched WI resources to their limits. Seven to eight hundred visitors were housed around the country after the conference and the 100 Norwegians, in their national costumes, arrived only at the last minute and expected to be housed in London – not easy for a country organization to arrange.

Like the WI, the ACWW is non-party and non-sectarian. Mrs Watt declared that 'When Country women of the world work together for common good, we can determine the direction of human history. Neither guns, nor gold, nor governments can contribute as much as, working together, we can do.' Their aims were idealistic and their expressions of view are still submitted to the appropriate agencies of the United Nations Organization.

Although they boast eight or nine million affiliated members, it is hard for ACWW to utilize this mass strength directly for any immediate purpose, beyond promoting general friendliness, goodwill and an exchange of views. Their greatest contribution is financial. Many local WIs, as well as organizations throughout the world, contribute to the 'pennies for friendship' scheme, started by Mrs Dorothy Drage on the principle that money could be elicited more easily by asking for very small amounts than by asking for large contributions.

With the support of this scheme, ACWW reported in 1974 that, among other things, 'Women in eighteen jungle villages in India were taught child care, nutrition, hygiene, cookery and literacy. Ceylon was able to equip 24 village welfare centres and buy equipment to train women in the art of everyday survival to pass on to their fellow countrywomen . . . Women in Uganda have been taught to read and write and take more part in local affairs. In Colombia, a child care centre has been set up to help hundreds of women draw a better life for their families from their surroundings. Landrovers and trained teaching and medical staff have been supplied in countries where roads are bad or non-existent. And, most recently, delegates at the 1972 Oslo Conference are pledged to finance a scheme to 'make means available for certain pilot projects in nutritional education in women with a special view to prevent blindness through ignorance''.' Mrs Olive Farquharson, a past vice-chairman of the National Federation, is the present world president of ACWW.

A world to care for

What reservations the WI held about ACWW remained only because of their own considerable international work. In 1952, the Malayan government invited the WI to lend an organizer for six months to start up a WI movement in that country. Margaret Herbertson flew out armed with basic visual aids on child care, hygiene, gardening, plain sewing and toy-making, resolved to initiate a basic pattern of WI life. A second representative was sent out when Miss Herbertson returned and their work in Malaya became the subject of world-wide interest.

Lady Templer, the wife of the high commissioner, reported that Miss Herbertson 'has worked tirelessly, giving all she can, incessantly travelling, staying in different places every night and never sparing herself . . . She has done a marvellous job out here.' Of the second representative, Viola Williams, Lady Templer said, 'When she arrived WIs were on a firm foundation but they were only a skeleton. When she left they were firmly established as a part of the pattern of Malayan life.' Among the dangers that Miss Williams faced were 'Red' roads, considered unsafe on account of being in areas known to hold active Communist terrorists. Lady Templer's conclusion was that, 'Women's Institutes in Malaya were a great adventure. When we started there were many prophecies of failure and few of success. Now we are constantly asked, "Why did no one think of this before?"'

Seven years later, the WI were concerned with the tragic fate of refugees throughout the world. 1959 was World Refugee Year. 'I know you will do all you can,' said Chairman Lady Dyer in her AGM address. The UK Committee set a provisional minimum target for the United Kingdom of £2 million, excluding government contributions.

On their own level, many WIs and some County Federations 'adopted' refugee families or even whole refugee camps. A policy to phase out these camps was inaugurated but inevitably they straggled on for some time. WIs were impressed with the importance of keeping up with their 'adopted' families for several years. It was no good, they were reminded, to let adoptions lapse after only a few months' interest. Money-raising efforts were strenuous.

The work was not entirely new to the WI. Yorkshire had already 'adopted' Rensberg camp in 1957, since when families and individuals had been taken under the wings of more than 34 local WIs. In addition, Yorkshire members raised £2000 in cash and sent 200 tea chests full of clothing and 'other comforts' to the camp. Twenty-four more tea chests were sent for Christmas with gifts ranging from cakes, sweets and tinned foods to hot water bottles, toys, new clothing, towels, soap and pillow slips. To provide first-hand knowledge of conditions, members and their husbands visited the camp.

The greatest fund-raising effort of all was on behalf of the Freedom From Hunger Campaign. Between 1962 and 1966, the WI raised the remarkable sum of £182,000. The WI markets raised another £3000 of their own to pay for the building and equipping of a trading store in a depressed area of what was then called Bechuanaland.

The place was Radisele, on the Bamangwato Development Association agricultural project, which was started in an attempt to improve farming methods and to organize village industry and trading for the benefit of the local community. Prior to the project, the land was on the edge of famine and the people apathetic. Stumps had to be cleared, land fenced and planted with crops of ground nuts, maize and millet. A cattle ranch was started. With the addition of the market, crops could be bought and stored against future famine and the local tribe could buy goods that previously had only been available from a small store seventeen miles away. Local producers had often had to travel up to thirty miles to the nearest town in order to sell their goods for cash.

Jam, salt and kerosene were most in demand at the Radisele market, although hardware, clothing, blankets, piece goods, agricultural equipment and general wares were also sold. The profits were literally ploughed back into the land. Another sort of profit quickly emerged, just as it does in the home markets: the store became a central meeting place, where ideas could be exchanged, methods of co-operation and improvement learnt and the life of the people enriched by human contact. News from Radisele continues to be full of activity. By the 1970s, the store had an annual turnover of £25,000. It is, incidentally, not the only international situation in which the markets helped out. In Zambia, today, WI markets have been able to demonstrate how to make six pairs of underpants from one yard of fabric – a commendable economy!

Meanwhile, the WI Freedom From Hunger Campaign started to raise £18,000 to build and equip a Farm Institute in Karamoja, Uganda – a conservation-orientated course aimed at post-primary education for boys and girls in their country's problems of over-grazing and erosion. Within a year, roughly half the WI had raised more than twice the required money and two more projects were undertaken. Five thousand pounds were set aside for the Lady Aberdeen scholarship fund to train suitable women from underdeveloped countries in nutrition and dietetics. The second project was a contribution to the development of a new University Farm in Trinidad.

In addition, five per cent of all funds received were sent to the UK Committee, to help with administration and publicity costs of its five-year effort. There were also projects in Ceylon, to help repair the fishing fleets after a disastrous cyclone had destroyed them all; in Sarawak, to which eighty buffaloes were imported to be trained as draught animals to increase the area of wet paddy fields; and in Rhodesia, where two jeeps were supplied to the WI sister organization to enable them to travel among the village women to teach literacy, health-care, nutrition and housecraft. The African women called the jeeps 'Jekesa Pfungwa' and 'Vuling Quondo', which both mean 'open the mind'.

Two other characters, Regent and Rudge, were exported by West Kent to Tristan da

Cunha to improve the island herd. Apparently the two bull calves 'settled down very quickly and were eating well'. Meanwhile, a Brahman bull was shipped over from Fiji to the British Solomon Islands, to improve another herd belonging to the Islands' college, to which the WI made a contribution of £10,000 to raise the agricultural teaching standards. A further contribution was made to a project in Colombia, which attempted to protect pre-school children from malnutrition. Sixteen nutritional recovery centres and sixty food demonstration units were opened by the government to combat the horrifying 90,000 annual child death rate.

Help to underdeveloped nations did not stop with the Freedom From Hunger Campaign. The WI are now dedicated to the Second United Nations Development Decade, or DD2, to discuss which they held their own conference under the title, 'A World to Share'. Representatives of the WI continue to attend triennial ACWW conferences, the last of which was in Perth, Australia. Grants were available for a limited time from the Foreign and Commonwealth Office to the counties to encourage co-operative projects with women in other European countries. Not surprisingly, entry into the Common Market has given added interest to involvement in Europe. *Home and Country* gave WI members a detailed account of how the EEC works, so that they could decide for themselves the benefits and problems.

True to their sex, they held an international conference entitled 'Keeping Ourselves Informed' to celebrate International Woman's Year. Truer still to their traditions, the WI did not send a representative to the highlighted Mexican jamboree at the end of the year. They preferred to get on with the work.

Even the smallest contribution helps. The last tale of international goodwill comes from Surrey, who made a special effort during the Freedom From Hunger Campaign to increase the export of cloves from the island of Zanzibar – upon which trade the island economy used largely to depend. A pomander competition was held. So great was the enthusiasm that many Surrey grocers ran clean out of cloves and had to re-order. No news from Zanzibar records island reaction to this trade boost.

THERE has been so much activity on so large a scale and for so long that it is only too easy to forget the million things done by local WIs that never get into the reports. No wonder they sometimes feel that the organization may have become a little too large for comfort. There's always the danger that the fun of WI membership, so important as a sound basis for collective energy, could become submerged under procedural business. Some members may be heard to murmur rebelliously, 'There's too much concern for *national* issues. What about us?'

They are quite right to insist on enjoying WI membership but wrong to assume that national issues do not concern them. Anyone who thinks of joining the WI is already busy enough, possibly sharing in many other aspects of local activity. The WI offers an enjoyable extra to village life and, through the WI, members of the village get to know their community, recognize its problems and combine to take action on their own behalf. A desire to *do* something follows on naturally from a sense of involvement in the community. In short, mutual involvement in the lighter side of life provides the impetus for more serious communal activity.

There is also great satisfaction to be had in relating local community issues to national concerns. It is the WI *national* organization that makes this important connection possible, although some members take a moment or two to recognize this.

Take, for instance, the broad implications of a recent national resolution on transport, which had to be discussed at what one local WI calls their 'boring' meeting of the year, before they proceed with their drama group or latest competition. In the same breath, the same local member recalls proudly how the village won a weekly bus from the local council by the

Looking to the future

efforts of the WI. On their own level, therefore, they *have* made a contribution to the national mandate. Their effort becomes part of a wider effort, which the NFWI co-ordinates throughout the country.

The issue of housing, in the abstract, sounds equally formidable. 'What can Headquarters expect *us* to do about the national housing problem?' But, when they thought about it, the same village *had* already done something. They had managed to get some derelicts done up by the council and stopped the building of a new row of useless boxes. The *national* problem can only be solved by *local* effort.

The weekly bus and the derelict houses were local issues. A local grievance repeated several thousand times by several thousand WIs represents a national issue. Some members may *sound* as if they're a little wary of the 'battling brigade' but more often than not they are conducting their own battles at their own level, which is how things get done.

The same association between local effort and national effort is made in the big competitions. The beautifully sculptored statuette of a horse or a delicately stitched binding to a book are things to be proud of in the home but, shown at a national exhibition before a public audience, they became articles of much greater value. A walk through the fields, noting their names, or a tally of trees in the neighbourhood make a nice day out but can also become an important survey of the country heritage.

It is easy to sympathize with local intolerance of the 'business' passed on to them from headquarters. 'There's not enough money for all the demands and who in the village has time for the paperwork!' But there is always the other side to the argument. 'Why won't the village WIs move faster, discuss *this* issue, block *that* absurd object, demand such-and-such a right? We must speak out at once if

In 1975 27-year-old Mrs Valerie Oxley became Firbeck cum Letwell's youngest president. Quite a change from that old image?

we're to use the strength of our membership. If members want all that Denman College offers, they must pay for it; if they want competitions, someone must organize them.'

A balanced life

The problems of money, the problems of time; conflict between the simpler requirements of the many and the complex needs of a busy organization that binds them together; the speed of the impetuous jerking at those who find everyday life active enough – those are the problems of any voluntary gathering of well-meaning, widely-drawn people. They spoke out once with vigour because they had a world to change and they helped to change it; now the world changes too fast and they find them-

119

selves delicately balanced between the whip and the brake.

Certain things they do agree about. 'Balance' was Mrs Watt's word – a vigorous, difficult woman, who brooked no compromise – balance between fun and social responsibility, between the interests of the villages and the necessities of organization. Lady Brunner thought that tolerance was the most important thing to be learnt – tolerance, pre-eminently, of each other's differences. The friction that occurs is the raw material upon which an understanding of balance and tolerance is built.

Pat Jacob believes that respect for the individual is a vital ingredient. 'However you combine to get things done,' she says, 'the individual must feel an important part of it. This is a way in which the WI can play a part in helping to maintain a society which does not become discordant.' Lady Dyer agrees: she thinks that the WI want everyone to count. 'Our greatest fear is that we shall cease to matter,' adds Mrs Hitchcock, once Lady Denman's secretary and formerly a national executive member.

'You know, in the old days we all knew each other but minded our own business,' an old man said to Mrs Pike's husband at a village party; 'now we all know each other's business but don't know each other.' 'Their activities mix,' says Miss Withall, once general secretary, 'but no longer their private lives.'

Nancy Tennant has faith in the continuity of the WI, which, she feels, gives it great strength. Its firm structure is what guarantees this continuity. 'The WI will survive,' said Miss Withall, 'because it fills a gap. It's withstood so many buffetings. It'll be here when we're all boxed.' Doris Cumming also believed that the WI provides continuity, 'in the past and for the future'. She wrote that they 'represent certain standards in national life', they are 'useful members of society, especially in rural areas, because they can be trained, within their own movement, to speak in public, conduct meetings, arrange public functions, judge competitive work, appreciate art, run a modern house, understand the problems of the old and the sick, and safeguard health'. They present, she added, 'a weight of simple fundamental reasoning based on a wide field'.

All this amounts to one thing above all that draws them together: democracy with humour, for they handle the complexities of democracy with a light touch and they remain one of the most painfully and pleasingly democratic organizations of which it is possible to conceive. Painful – because of the unwieldy nature and disparate elements of democracy. Pleasing – because most of us still want to believe in the ultimate efficacy of democracy.

Writing in 1940, in the midst of war, Margaret Hitchcock confessed that opponents of democracy objected that it was slow in action and that the machinery necessary for its working was cumbersome – a fair criticism of the WI. In answer to her own challenge, she added that slowness was itself a merit that gave people time to receive adequate information and to discuss it fully. As for the machinery, she saw the ballot as a very necessary part of the freedom of the democratic nation. 'The greatest degree of self-development is only possible under a democratic government,' she wrote, 'because under no other system can every adult think, speak and vote as he likes.'

Five years later – five years in which European democracy was on the verge of collapse – Lady Denman spoke out on its behalf. 'Democracy is slow off the mark, often cumbersome and frets the ardent spirit,' she said. 'It produces few reforms overnight and tolerates too long evils which a high-minded autocrat might abolish in an afternoon. But, nevertheless, it can accomplish miracles . . .'

Democracy is still the greatest strength and the greatest weakness of the WI. In 1974, the WI presented its evidence to the Wolfenden Committee on Voluntary Organizations. It spoke again of slowness of response to government legislation, of voluntary workers with less and less time to spare, of too many details and too little long-term planning, of the difficulties experienced in trying to dovetail the vision of the national WI with the will of the local WI, of generation gaps that caused WIs to split in two, of inborn resistance to increases in membership fees necessary to assure survival, of the possibility of decentralization.

All these are justified and important criticisms. As part of a democratic organization, it is up to WI members themselves to face the problems and overcome them. The consequences of not doing so would indirectly affect us all. If the WI cannot move fast enough to comment on government legislation, the pace of which is rapidly increasing, then it will no longer be able to sustain the value of its watching brief on our standards of life. If members don't pay their way, they won't be able to support the continuity of their own structure, hence the importance of the 1976 mandate that has altered the methods of raising the subscription. If they don't manage to find time for the WI as well as for their work, then the WI will fail to keep in touch with the truly representative voice of the people. And the meaning of democracy will be sadly misunderstood if members think it is anything less than an arena in which opposite viewpoints can safely spar.

Moreover, it is important that the WI does not get bogged down with its own problems. It must continue to look outside itself. Both Pat Jacob and the general secretary, Anne Ballard, regard involvement with the EEC as an essential extension of WI work and both would like to see the same sort of mutual representation between the WI and committees in Brussels as there is at present between the WI and government committees in this country. Only in that way can the WI continue to serve the interests of the community and maintain its concern for our welfare. If decisions about our future are being made in Brussels, then it is those decisions to which the WI must listen carefully.

The days when the WI were considered 'worthy women making wine and woad' are long past. If their image has been confused, that is because they represent such a wide cross-section of people and their activities are so broad that it would be as simple to produce an image of an entire society. Their numbers are necessarily limited by certain factors but those numbers are nevertheless impressive, and the limiting factors are steadily disappearing. Although the WI is a country organization, it is now moving into high-rise flats and housing estates; although it is a woman's organization, more and more things are done alongside men; and although it is primarily a group organization, the 'loner' is always respected.

Their numbers will certainly increase, if the need to economize lures more people to take an interest in the local scene and to become producers themselves as well as consumers. The WI is there to give them every opportunity to fulfil that interest and to take some pride in their locality as well as in wider issues. The combination of their activities and the sum of all they have achieved defines them as an organization which will continue to be an asset to the life of the nation.

The exercise of power

But if they are so large and their concerns are so wide, ask critics as well as sympathizers, accustomed to the more blatant demonstration of muscle popular among large and zealously committed organizations, then why don't the WI *use* their power? The answer is that they do but not in an obvious political sense.

Power in the WI is exercised by the constant application of pressure and by reasoned argument. They reflect the deep-rooted belief of most people that it ought to be possible, for instance, to devise a sensible rural bus-service without making it a political issue. More direct, political action of the kind that is sometimes urged on them by even the most well-meaning critics could in fact diminish their influence. For they hold a trusted position as the wise voice of ordinary reflective people and any demonstration of aggressive strength would erode that position. There are more subtle and more effective forces at work in a liberated democracy than many affirmers of the 'liberated' movements will sometimes allow. The WI, in their own surprising way, are one such force.

Mrs Jacob would see the WI – and she would be right – as the perfect channel for the woman who wants to be liberated in fact as well as in theory. Whether she wants to grow her own cabbages, service her car, knit herself a jump-suit or agitate for a creche for her babies, then the WI will train her in the subtle skills of committee activities, through which democracy acts. If she wishes to help make large, self-interested power groups responsive to the average, commonsense needs of ordinary citizens, or tackle the bureaucratic tendencies of, for instance, the Eurocrats, then through the WI she will learn how to speak out for her

Looking to the future

beliefs. She will also be able to link up with other women's organizations in Europe.

That *is* the exercise of power but of power within the framework of democracy. There is no brash exposure of muscle but, nevertheless, things get done. Fashionable platforms are no concern of the WI but the fundamental values for which the WI stands – the self-help and community action which the WI have promoted for sixty years – have brought them, with a full turn of the wheel, into the forefront of modern, positive social thinking. The contemporary urge is towards the very sort of community activity and interest at local level which was the original motivation for the WI.

Speaking in the clear idiom of today, they are determined to remain democratic and to represent all those in this democratic nation who are not members. Their concerns are the concerns of all of us. Upon their decisions and their action depends to a considerable extent the welfare of the individual in society. Upon their influence depends to an even greater extent the welfare of tomorrow's families, whom they are creating and for whom they are preparing.

Winning finalists of the 1976 NFWI/Green Shield Championship at Queen's Club, London, are Mrs Ann Firkin (left) of Bledington WI, Oxfordshire, and Mrs Wendy Wright of Milton and Wychwood WI, Oxfordshire. The Championship has become one of the most exciting events on the WI sporting calendar.

A WI DATE GUIDE

1897 February 19: First Women's Institute in the world formed at Stoney Creek, Ontario, Canada.

1915 September 11: First Women's Institute in England and Wales formed at Llanfair P.G., Anglesey, Wales.

1917 September: First County Federation formed (Sussex).
October: First Annual General Meeting of WI delegates; National Federation of Women's Institutes formed; subscription two shillings.
Lady Denman first chairman of NFWI.

1918 First National Handicraft Exhibition.
Voluntary County Organizers appointed and first VCO training school.

1919 March: First number of *Home and Country* published.
Consultative Council set up.
General Endowment Fund started.
The NFWI becomes self-governing.

1920 Guild of Learners of Handicrafts formed (Handicrafts Guild).
Grant of £10,000 made by Development Commissioners.

1922 Handicrafts Exhibition at Victoria and Albert Museum.

1923 Formation of Welsh Counties Conference.
Annual General Meeting decided that WI membership is open to women and girls only.

1926 NFWI's claim for exemption from Income Tax allowed on appeal.
Board of Education White Paper commends WIs.

1927 Financial Independence of NFWI.
Membership reaches 250,000.
Home and Country reaches 50,000 copies.

1928 First Drama Festival
First Report on the Constitution.
Denman Report on the education of girls in the country.

1929 National Council of Social Services requests NFWI to help unemployed.

1932 Annual General Meeting decided that the fares of all the delegates to the meeting should be pooled.
Resolution to organize and increase WI Co-operative Markets: Carnegie UK Trust Grant awarded for three years.

Mother and daughter at a Denman College course on carving in wood and stone.

1933 Number of WIs passes 5000 mark.
Associated Country Women of the World started.
Second Drama Festival.

1934 NFWI delegate to International Peace Conference in Geneva.

1937 The WI celebrate their twenty-first birthday.

1939 Produce Guild formed.
WIs help in evacuation scheme.
First grant from Development Commissioners for agricultural work.

1940 First grant from Ministry of Food; NFWI begins to administer Ministry of Food's fruit preservation scheme.

1943 Only wartime Annual General Meeting; decision made to adopt linking system because of size of movement.

1945 AGM instructed NF Executive Committee to establish a WI College.

1946 Lady Albemarle elected chairman on Lady Denman's retirement.
First Combined Arts Festival.
Home and Country reaches 100,000 copies.
CUKT grant to start WIs in Channel Islands.

1947 Operation Produce.

1948 Denman College opened.
First grant received from the Ministry of Education 'for the development of liberal education for women'.
Home Produce Exhibition.
Second Report on the Constitution.

1949 First WI in the Isle of Man formed.

1950 First Singing Festival: 'Folk Songs of the Four Seasons'.
Publication of 'Your Village' survey by WI.

1951 Lady Brunner elected chairman.
First Market Place at Ideal Home Exhibition, Olympia.
Festival of Britain celebrations.

1952 Crafts Exhibition at Victoria and Albert Museum.
Malayan Government invites WI representative to start Malayan WIs.

1953 Number of WIs passes 8000 mark.

1955 Keep Britain Tidy Group formed.

1956 Lady Dyer elected chairman.
WI membership reaches peak of over 462,000.

1957 Drama Festival: 'Out of this Wood'.

1958 Market Place at Ideal Home Exhibition, Olympia.

1959 Dame Frances Farrer resigns from the post of general secretary after thirty years.
WI contributes to World Refugee Year.

1961 Mrs G. L. S. Pike elected chairman.
Market Place at Ideal Home Exhibition, Olympia.
Resolution pledging WIs to support the Freedom From Hunger Campaign.

1962 Mrs Pike visits the Soviet Union.
Country Feasts and Festivals Competition at Dairy Show.

1963 First National Art Exhibition, 'Painting for Pleasure' at the Galleries of the Federation of British Artists.
First WI in psychiatric hospital.

1964 *Home and Country* reaches 150,000 copies.

1965 Golden Jubilee Year.
'Golden Market Place', Ideal Home Exhibition, Olympia.
Rule limiting formation of WIs to places with under 4000 population rescinded.
WI 'Scrapbooks of the Countryside'.

1966 WI Freedom from Hunger fund closed at £182,000.
National Appeal for half a million pounds launched.
Lady Anglesey elected chairman.
WI involvement in Stop Accidents Year.
Nearly 9000 WIs by the end of the year.

1969 Miss Sylvia Gray elected chairman.
First performance in the Royal Albert Hall of 'The Brilliant and the Dark'.
Aim of National Appeal (over £500,000) realized.

1970 Third report on the constitution.
CUKT grant awarded to launch Town and Country project.
WI involvement in European Conservation Year.

1971 Resolution passed at AGM changing the interpretation of the non-party political and non-sectarian rules.
WI member Mrs O. Farquharson elected World President of ACWW.

1972 'This Green and Pleasant Land?' Exhibition at Ideal Home Exhibition, Olympia.
Produce and Handicrafts Guilds ceased, replaced by Home Economics courses open to all members.

1974 Mrs Pat Jacob elected chairman.
Report to Wolfenden Committee on Voluntary Organizations.

1975 Diamond Jubilee.
WI involvement in European Architectural Heritage Year.
'Tomorrow's Heirlooms' exhibition.

1976 Approval of new methods of charging the subscription.

WE WISH TO THANK

The publishers would like to thank all those WI members who responded to their appeal for photographs and letters. They regret that there was space only to include some of them. We also wish to credit Keystone, Greater London Council, Home and Country, Press Association and research assistant Stephanie Ross.